PROFESSIONALLY AND PERSONALLY POLISHED

Learn Clear and Confident Communication in Every Aspect of Life

Samuel N. Anene

I am wholeheartedly dedicating this book to my mum, Mrs. Nkechi Anene.

AUTHOR'S NOTE

Dear Communicator:

Thank you for picking up *Professionally and Personally Polished*. This book is special to me. I would like you to view it, not just as a book, but also as a personal letter from me to you. In simpler terms, it was written with you in mind.

You see, as a child, I was as timid as a mouse-my heart would race at the thought of speaking in front of others, making me avoid the spotlight at all costs. Growing up, I experienced extreme ridicule from people who listened to my speech, on several occasions. One time, an extended family member told me that I was sluggish.

When I set out to write *Professionally and Personally Polished*, I was not just thinking about emails, presentations, or meetings. I was thinking about the everyday conversations that shape our lives—at work, at home, and in our most personal relationships. Communication is at the heart of everything we do, and I have experienced firsthand how mastering it can open doors to success and strengthen our most important connections.

This book is born out of my passion for helping people communicate better, not just in their careers, but in every aspect of their lives. As someone who has spent years teaching, coaching, and learning the nuances of language, I have seen how powerful the right words can be. I also know how frustrating it can feel when we struggle to express ourselves or understand others, whether in a business meeting or a conversation with a loved one.

Professionally and Personally Polished is more than a guide; it is a toolkit for navigating both the professional world and personal relationships with clarity, confidence, and grace.

My hope is that as you turn these pages, you'll find strategies that resonate with your everyday life, helping you to communicate with impact, no matter the context. Here's to your success—both professionally and personally.

Warm Regards,

Samuel N. Anene

INTRODUCTION

Welcome to *Professionally and Personally Polished*, a book that will guide you through the art of effective communication, whether you are addressing a crowd, holding a one-to-one conversation, or simply writing an important message. Communication is the foundation of everything we do, and this book will help you sharpen those skills in a way that feels natural, authentic, and impactful.

Throughout these pages, you will explore the essential foundations of communication—understanding the process of how messages are sent, received, and interpreted. You will also find insights into interpersonal communication, helping you handle conversations with tact, empathy, and clarity. Public speaking, which can be daunting for many, is broken down into simple, manageable steps, so that you can express yourself confidently in front of any audience.

Whether you are writing business emails or casual texts, this book covers the dos and don'ts of written communication, ensuring that your message always comes across clearly and professionally. For those in the fitness world, there is even a special section dedicated to English for fitness professionals, so that you can speak the language of motivation, instruction, and encouragement with precision.

We will also consider commonly misused expressions in English, particularly focusing on phrases that can be confusing for Nigerian speakers. You will find yourself nodding along as you recognise some of the tricky phrases that often slip into everyday conversations, and you will learn how to use them correctly.

At its core, *Professionally and Personally Polished* is about helping you refine your communication skills in every area of your life. Whether in the boardroom, a social gathering, or a casual chat, the ability to express yourself clearly and confidently is invaluable.

So, let us begin this journey together. I hope you find this book to be not just a guide, but a helpful companion as you work towards becoming polished in both your professional and personal life.

TABLE OF CONTENTS

Dedication.. ii

Author's note iii

Introduction.. iv

CHAPTER 1: FOUNDATIONS OF COMMUNICATION 1

Understanding the Communication Process:.................................... 1
The Difference Between Verbal and Non-Verbal Communication 2
Active Listening Skills 3

CHAPTER 2: INTERPERSONAL COMMUNICATION 5

How to Respond to Passive-Aggressive Comments.............................. 5
Dealing With Interruptions During Conversations 6
How to Disagree with Civility 6
How to Handle Heated Conversations 9
How to Handle Criticism Constructively 9
Setting Boundaries in Personal and Professional Relationships 10
Navigating Sensitive Topics Without Offending.................................. 11
Dealing with Someone Who Always Wants to Be Right 11
Handling Silent Treatment in Conflict Situations............................... 12
How to Stay Calm and Composed Under Pressure............................... 13
How to Handle Sensitive Topics Without Offending............................ 14
How to Respond When Someone Disrespects Your Boundaries 15
How to Handle Bad Apologies... 16
How to Apologise Sincerely and Effectively....................................... 17
Dealing with People Who Play the Victim... 18
How to Respond to Gaslighting... 19
How to Respond When They Say You're Being Too Sensitive.................. 20
Responding to Overly Defensive Behaviour.. 21
How to Respond to Fake Compliments 21
How to Assert Your Needs Without Feeling Guilty............................... 23
Responding to Unsolicited Advice... 24
Dealing with People Who Dismiss Your Feelings 25
Dealing with Someone Who Always Wants to Be Right 27
How to Avoid Taking Things Personally in Arguments.......................... 28
How to Stop Apologising Excessively in Conversations 29
How to Respond to Public Criticism.. 30
How to Respond to Gaslighting... 31
How to Address Sarcasm Without Being Defensive.............................. 33
How to Manage Conflicts with Manipulative People 34
Recognising When to Walk Away from a Conflict................................ 35

How to Respond When Somebody Tells a Lie 37
How to Avoid Overthinking Conflict Situations.............................. 38
Recognizing and Avoiding Emotional Triggers............................... 39
How to Handle Emotional Blackmail in Relationships................... 41
How to Stop Stonewalling in Arguments 42
How to Disengage from Toxic Conversations 43
How to Keep Your Cool When Provoked.. 45
How to Manage Your Tone During Difficult Conversations 46
How to Navigate Conversations with Overly Emotional People.... 47

CHAPTER 3: COMMUNICATION AND SOCIAL SKILLS...................... **49**

30 Sophisticated Conversation Starters 53

CHAPTER 4: PUBLIC SPEAKING.. **55**

Struggling With Stage Fright.. 55
Why You Fear Public Speaking 56
What You Are Doing Wrong.. 59
Avoid These Pitfalls When Addressing Your Audience................... 60
Steps For Improving Ability As A Speaker 62
BONUS: How To Prepare Your Speech 83

CHAPTER 5: BUSINESS WRITING... **85**

Understanding the Purpose of Business Writing............................ 85
Effective Writing: What to Do vs. What to Avoid 89
Crafting a Polished Professional Email... 92
How To Write Reports, Memos, And Proposals, Like A Professional....... 99

CHAPTER 6: WORKPLACE ETIQUETTE... **112**

Why Compliments on Appearance Don't Belong in the Workplace 112
What to do When Gathering Your Thoughts 115
Customer Service... 117

CHAPTER 7: GRAMMAR... **124**

Commonly Misused Expressions by Nigerian Speakers 124

CONCLUSION **188**

CHAPTER 1

FOUNDATIONS OF COMMUNICATION

The title *Foundations of Communication* reflects the basic yet powerful elements that shape how we connect with others. In this section, we will consider what makes communication effective, covering everything from how messages are sent and received to the impact of both verbal and non-verbal cues. We will also explore the importance of active listening—because truly hearing someone can make all the difference. By understanding these essentials, you will be better prepared to build lasting connections, whether in personal interactions or professional environments.

The communication process is the framework that explains how information flows between individuals. It involves several key components:

Understanding the Communication Process:

Sender: This is the person who initiates the communication. The sender has a thought, idea, or piece of information they want to convey to someone else. It starts with the sender's intention to communicate something, which is then encoded into a message. Encoding simply means putting thoughts into words, gestures, or symbols that the receiver can understand.

Message: The message is the actual content of the communication. It could be spoken words, a written text, or even a gesture. The message should be clear and structured so that the receiver understands it as intended. However, what complicates things is that sometimes the message sent is not always the message received, which is why clarity is so important.

Medium: The medium is how the message is transmitted from the sender to the receiver. This could be a conversation, an email, a phone call, or even body language. Choosing the right medium depends on the context. For example, sensitive topics might be better discussed face-to-face rather than through a text message.

Receiver: The receiver is the person who receives and interprets the message. The receiver's background, emotions, and experiences influence how they interpret the message, which is why what you mean and what they understand can sometimes differ.

Feedback: Feedback is the response from the receiver, which lets the sender know whether the message was understood correctly. It could be a verbal reply, a facial expression, or even silence. Feedback completes the communication loop because it allows the sender to adjust or clarify the message if needed.

The Difference Between Verbal and Non-Verbal Communication:

Communication is not just about words. In fact, a significant part of communication happens without words. Let us break down these two types:

Verbal Communication

This is the use of words to convey a message. It includes both spoken and written communication. Verbal communication allows us to articulate ideas, give instructions, and express feelings. It is precise and direct, but it relies heavily on the choice of words and clarity. For example, saying "I appreciate your help" is a verbal expression of gratitude.

Non-Verbal Communication

This involves body language, facial expressions, tone of voice, posture, gestures, and even eye contact. Non-verbal cues can reinforce what you are saying or completely contradict it. For example, saying "I am happy to see you" with a frown will confuse the listener because your words and body language are not aligned. Non-verbal communication is crucial because people tend to trust what they see more than what they hear. It often communicates emotions and attitudes even more effectively than words.

Understanding the balance between verbal and non-verbal communication helps ensure your message is received as you intend it.

Active Listening Skills:

Listening is often taken for granted, but active listening is a skill that can transform how we communicate. It goes beyond simply hearing words; it involves fully engaging with the speaker to understand their message on a deeper level. Here are the components of active listening:

FOCUS

Active listening means giving the speaker your full attention, free from distractions. This includes maintaining eye contact, not interrupting, and showing interest in what is being said. This kind of attention reassures the speaker that you are present and value what they are saying.

UNDERSTANDING

It is important to make an effort to understand the message, not just the words but the emotions and intentions behind them. Sometimes, a person may not express their feelings directly, and active listening helps you pick up on these unspoken cues.

FEEDBACK

Providing thoughtful feedback is a core part of active listening. It could be verbal, like asking follow-up questions or summarising what the speaker has said to show that you are tracking the conversation. Non-verbal feedback — like nodding, smiling, or maintaining eye contact—also reinforces that you are engaged.

CLARIFICATION

If something is unclear, active listening involves asking questions to clarify the meaning. For example, you might say, "Just to be sure I understand, are you saying that...?" This ensures that there are no misunderstandings and that both parties are on the same page.

Listening with empathy means trying to put yourself in the other person's shoes and understand things from their perspective. It is about showing that you care about what they are saying, even if you do not necessarily agree with them.

INTERPERSONAL COMMUNICATION

Interpersonal communication is simply how we exchange information, thoughts, or feelings with others. It happens when we talk, listen, use body language, or even text. It is a two-way street where both people actively send and receive messages, trying to understand each other. The goal is usually to connect, build relationships, or get a point across. Think of it like a conversation where both sides matter equally—whether you are chatting with a friend, giving advice, or negotiating a deal! Let us consider various aspects of interpersonal communication.

How to Respond to Passive-Aggressive Comments

When someone makes a passive-aggressive comment, it can feel like a hidden insult wrapped in politeness. The key to responding is to address the behaviour directly without taking the bait, keeping things calm and constructive.

WHEN THEY SAY:

"I'm not shocked you're acting this way," it is a clear dig at your character or past behaviour, subtly accusing you of being predictable in a negative way. It can feel like an insult disguised as an observation. Here are five ways to handle it:

HOW TO RESPOND:

- *"I'm not sure what you mean by that, but let's focus on the real issue here. What's bothering you?"*

- *"I feel uncomfortable when I hear comments like that. Can we talk about it directly?"*

- *"What do you mean by that? I'd prefer if we address the issue directly."*

- *I feel like that comment is pointing fingers, and I'd rather talk openly about what's going on. What's really the issue here?"*

- *"If something I've done is frustrating you, I'd appreciate it if you told me directly so we can address it."*

Dealing With Interruptions During Conversations

When you are being interrupted, it is important to respond in a way that reclaims your speaking time without causing conflict. Here are three things you can say:

- ***"I'd like to finish my point, if that's okay."***
  This is polite but direct, reminding the other person that you haven't finished speaking and asking for their patience.

- ***"Hold on a second, let me just complete what I was saying."***
  This acknowledges the interruption and politely signals that you're not done yet.

- ***"I'll give you a chance to respond, but let me finish my thought first."***
  This assures the person that they'll get their turn but reinforces that you need to complete your idea first.

- ***"I see you're eager to jump in, but I just need to finish my thought first."***

- ***"I wasn't finished speaking, let me just complete my point."***

How to Disagree with Civility

Oftentimes, I see people express their disagreement by using insults or dismissive remarks, which not only escalates tension but also shuts down meaningful dialogue. This approach might make the person feel like they have "won" the argument, but it usually damages relationships and creates a hostile environment. Disagreeing with civility, on the other hand, allows for productive discussions where different perspectives can be shared

without undermining respect. Let us consider a few things to bear in mind when you have a different perspective on an issue or idea.

- *"I see your point, but I think we should consider…"*

  Example: "I see your point about increasing our marketing budget, but I think we should consider the current economic climate."

- *"That's an interesting perspective, however…"*

  Example: "That's an interesting perspective on expanding to new markets, however, we might face logistical challenges."

- *"I understand where you're coming from, but…"*

  Example: "I understand where you're coming from with the new policy, but it might not be well-received by our staff."

- *"I appreciate your idea, though I believe…"*

  Example: "I appreciate your idea to extend working hours, though I believe it could affect employee morale."

- *"While I respect your opinion, I think…"*

  Example: "While I respect your opinion on outsourcing, I think we should focus on building our in-house team."

- *"That's a valid point, but we might also want to consider…"*

  Example: "That's a valid point about the new software, but we might also want to consider its compatibility with our existing systems."

- *"I see what you're saying, yet I feel…"*

  Example: "I see what you're saying about the new project timeline, yet I feel it might be too ambitious given our current resources."

A few other important points to note include the following:

- STAY CALM AND COMPOSED

  In moments of strong disagreement, emotions can run high. Take a moment to breathe and gather your thoughts before responding.

Keeping your cool helps prevent the conversation from turning into a heated argument.

- ### Separate the Person from the Issue

Focus on the topic at hand, not the individual. This helps prevent the disagreement from becoming personal. Make it clear that your criticism is about the idea, not the person.

Example: **"I respect your experience, but I have concerns about the effectiveness of this approach."**

- ### Use Empathy

Try to understand where the other person is coming from, even if you disagree. Acknowledging their feelings or concerns can help de-escalate tension.

Example: **"I see that this issue is really important to you, and I appreciate your passion. My perspective is a bit different..."**

- ### Find Points of Agreement

Even in strong disagreements, there are often areas where you can agree. Highlighting these can create a foundation for constructive dialogue.

Example: **"We both want what's best for the project, though we have different ideas on how to achieve it."**

- ### Agree to Disagree if Necessary

Sometimes, consensus is not possible, and that is okay. If the disagreement remains unresolved, it is perfectly acceptable to agree to disagree and move forward respectfully.

Example: **"It seems we're at an impasse on this. Let's agree to disagree and consider both perspectives moving forward."**

- ### Consider Taking a Break

If the conversation becomes too heated, suggest taking a break. Stepping away allows everyone to cool down and approach the discussion later with a clearer mind.

- FOCUS ON SOLUTIONS, NOT WINNING

  The goal of a strong disagreement should be to find a resolution or a better understanding, not to "win" the argument. Keep the conversation solution-oriented.

How to Handle Heated Conversations

When tempers flare during a conversation, it is easy to say things you do not mean or let the situation spiral. Managing your anger is key to keeping things productive rather than destructive.

TAKE A BREATHER

If you feel yourself getting worked up, it is totally fine to take a step back. Something like, *"I need a moment to gather my thoughts,"* can give you that pause to calm down before you say something you might regret.

FOCUS ON THE ISSUE, NOT THE PERSON

Keep the conversation about the problem, not the person. Instead of saying, *"You're always doing this!"* you could say, *"I'm frustrated by how this situation is playing out."* It takes the personal sting out of it.

- Use "I" Statements: Blame never goes well. Instead of pointing fingers, try saying, *"I feel upset when I'm interrupted, and I'd like to finish what I was saying."* It keeps things about your experience and not an attack on them.

- Breathe and Slow Down: When emotions are high, slow down the pace. Take a deep breath, speak a bit slower—it helps keep the conversation calm and thoughtful.

Advice? **Keeping your cool in the heat of the moment is powerful. When you manage your anger, you take control of the situation instead of letting it control you.**

How to Handle Criticism Constructively

Criticism is never fun, but it doesn't have to feel like an attack. It can actually be a chance to learn and grow—if you let it.

LISTEN WITHOUT DEFENSIVENESS:

The instinct is to defend yourself, but hold off for a second. Just listen first. Try saying, *"I hear you; can you tell me more about what you mean?"* That way, they feel heard, and you get a clearer idea of their feedback.

ASK FOR SPECIFICS

If the feedback is too vague, ask for examples. You could say, *"Could you give me an example of when that happened?"* That way, it's easier to see what they're really talking about.

THANK THEM FOR THEIR FEEDBACK

I know, it sounds tough, but thanking someone for their criticism shows maturity. You could say, *"Thanks for sharing that, I'll think about how I can work on it."* It's a graceful way to handle it.

REFLECT BEFORE RESPONDING

Before you jump to conclusions or get defensive, take a minute to think. Sometimes there's value in the feedback, and sometimes you'll realise it's off the mark.

Advice? **Criticism does not have to knock you down. If you can listen and take what is helpful from it, it becomes a tool for growth, not a source of stress.**

Setting Boundaries in Personal and Professional Relationships

Boundaries are like invisible lines that protect your peace of mind, your time, and your energy. Here is how to set them, without feeling guilty.

BE CLEAR AND DIRECT:

People cannot respect boundaries they do not know exist. So be upfront. At work, it could be something like, *"I don't respond to work messages after 6 p.m."* In your personal life, you might say, *"I need time to unwind after work before we talk about anything serious."*

Once you have set a boundary, stick to it. If someone crosses it, remind them. For example, *"Hey, we agreed not to discuss this here, remember?"* Being consistent helps people respect your limits.

DON'T FEEL GUILTY

Boundaries are about taking care of yourself, not shutting people out. It is okay to say no and protect your time. You are not being selfish; you are making sure you can show up as your best self.

ENFORCE CONSEQUENCES

If someone keeps ignoring your boundaries, do not be afraid to take action. You can say, *"If this keeps happening, I'll need to step back from these conversations."* Sometimes, enforcing consequences is the only way to protect your space.

Navigating Sensitive Topics Without Offending

"I'd like to discuss something that's been on my mind, but I want to be mindful of your feelings. Can we have an open conversation?"

"I'm not sure how to bring this up without causing offence, but I think it's important we talk about it."

"I want to be respectful while sharing my thoughts. Please let me know if I'm stepping into sensitive territory."

"This is a tricky subject, and I want to approach it with care. How do you feel about us discussing it?"

"I'm bringing this up because it matters to me, but I respect your perspective. Let's keep it respectful as we talk."

Dealing with Someone Who Always Wants to Be Right

Interacting with someone who insists on being right can be frustrating, but responding with sarcasm or dismissiveness often makes things worse. The aim is to keep the conversation respectful and focus on finding common ground. Avoid making the other person feel attacked or belittled.

"You always have to be right, don't you?"

WHY IT SHOULD NOT BE SAID: This is confrontational and puts the other person on the defensive, making it harder to have a productive conversation.

"You know what? Whatever. You win."
WHY IT SHOULD NOT BE SAID: This sounds dismissive and sarcastic, which can escalate the situation instead of resolving it.

"This is pointless because you think you're perfect."
WHY IT SHOULD NOT BE SAID: This is accusatory and will likely make the person dig in their heels rather than listen.

WHAT TO SAY INSTEAD:

"You've made a good point, but I see things a little differently. Can we consider both perspectives?"

"I get where you're coming from, but let's agree that we might not have all the answers right now."

"It seems like we're not on the same page, and that's okay. How about we find a compromise?"

"I respect your opinion, and I think we can both bring something valuable to the conversation."

"It's not about who's right or wrong. Let's focus on finding a solution that works for both of us."

Handling Silent Treatment in Conflict Situations

The silent treatment can be emotionally draining, but responding with anger or accusations can deepen the divide. Instead, it is best to express empathy and a desire to understand. Avoid saying anything that dismisses their feelings or makes them feel pressured to respond immediately.

"Why are you acting so childish? Just talk to me."
WHY IT SHOULD NOT BE SAID: Labelling their behaviour as childish is insulting and dismissive, which will likely make them more resistant to communication.

"Fine, if you don't want to talk, I'm done too."

WHY IT SHOULD NOT BE SAID: This sounds like giving up on the relationship and adds to the emotional distance, making reconciliation harder.

"You're being immature by not responding."

WHY IT SHOULD NOT BE SAID: Calling someone immature puts them in a negative light and can make them retreat further into silence.

WHAT TO SAY INSTEAD:

"I notice you've been quiet, and I'm not sure what's on your mind. Can we talk about what's bothering you?"

"It feels like something's off between us. I'm here to listen whenever you're ready to talk."

"I'd really like to understand your side of things. Silence can make things harder to resolve."

"I value our relationship, and I don't want to leave things unresolved. How can we work through this?"

"I know things are tense, but avoiding the conversation won't help us. Let's try to address this calmly."

How to Stay Calm and Composed Under Pressure

In high-pressure situations, it is easy to let frustration take over. However, losing your temper or panicking can make the situation worse. It is important to avoid language that escalates stress or shows that you are overwhelmed.

"This is too much! I can't handle it."
WHY IT SHOULD NOT BE SAID: This reinforces the feeling of being overwhelmed and may cause others to panic as well.

"You're stressing me out, just stop!"
WHY IT SHOULD NOT BE SAID: This puts the blame on others and can make them feel guilty or defensive, which increases tension.

"This is a disaster; everything's falling apart!"
WHY IT SHOULD NOT BE SAID: This amplifies the stress and negativity, making it harder to find a calm way out.

WHAT TO SAY INSTEAD:

"Let me take a moment to gather my thoughts before we continue. I want to approach this calmly."

"I understand this is stressful, but we'll get through it one step at a time. Let's focus on the next best move."

"It's important we don't rush decisions under pressure. Let's take a breath and figure this out together."

"I can see this is a tense situation, but panicking won't help. I'll keep my cool so we can find a solution."

"We've been through challenges before, and we made it work. Let's stay composed and work through this."

How to Handle Sensitive Topics Without Offending

Discussing sensitive topics requires care and thoughtfulness. The goal is to express your point without making the other person feel attacked or uncomfortable. Avoid blunt statements or phrasing that suggests you don't care about their feelings.

WHAT NOT TO SAY:

"I don't care if this offends you, but I have to say it."
WHY IT SHOULD NOT BE SAID: This dismisses the other person's emotions and signals that you are more focused on your own thoughts than their feelings.

"I'm just being honest. You need to hear the truth."
Why it should not be said: While honesty is important, this phrase can come off as abrasive and makes it seem like you're preparing to criticise harshly.

"I don't see why you'd be sensitive about this, but here goes."
Why it should not be said: Dismissing the other person's potential sensitivity shows a lack of empathy and makes it harder for them to open up.

What to say instead:

"I'd like to discuss something that's been on my mind, but I want to be mindful of your feelings. Can we have an open conversation?"

"I'm not sure how to bring this up without causing offence, but I think it's important we talk about it."

"I want to be respectful while sharing my thoughts. Please let me know if I'm stepping into sensitive territory."

"This is a tricky subject, and I want to approach it with care. How do you feel about us discussing it?"

"I'm bringing this up because it matters to me, but I respect your perspective. Let's keep it respectful as we talk."

How to Respond When Someone Disrespects Your Boundaries

Setting boundaries is essential in maintaining respect in both romantic and professional settings. However, when someone disrespects those boundaries, it's important to stand your ground without lashing out or apologising for asserting yourself.

What not to say:

"I guess it's okay, just this once..."
Why it should not be said: It weakens your stance and encourages further boundary violations by making it seem like your boundaries are flexible.

"Why do you always cross my boundaries?!"
WHY IT SHOULD NOT BE SAID: This sounds accusatory and can escalate the situation, making the other person defensive rather than reflective.

"Forget it, it's not a big deal."
WHY IT SHOULD NOT BE SAID: This dismisses the issue and allows the other person to ignore your boundaries without consequences.

WHAT TO SAY INSTEAD:

"I've made my boundaries clear, and it's important that they're respected. I need us to stick to that."

"When my boundaries are crossed, it makes me feel like my needs aren't being valued. Let's ensure this doesn't happen again."

"I'd appreciate it if you could be more mindful of my boundaries moving forward."

"It's crucial that we both respect each other's limits for this relationship to work."

"I'm happy to work with you on this, but my boundaries aren't negotiable."

How to Handle Bad Apologies

Sometimes people give insincere or half-hearted apologies, either because they don't fully understand the impact of their actions or because they're trying to avoid accountability. Responding with grace helps you maintain your composure while still addressing the issue.

WHAT NOT TO SAY:

"Whatever, forget about it."
WHY IT SHOULD NOT BE SAID: This dismisses the issue and allows the person to think that their apology (or lack thereof) was sufficient, even if it was not.

"This is why I don't bother telling you when something's wrong!"
WHY IT SHOULD NOT BE SAID: This makes it about past grievances rather than the current issue, derailing the conversation and escalating tension.

"I appreciate you acknowledging this, but I'd like to hear more about what steps you'll take moving forward."

"Thanks for apologising. I'd like us to talk more about how we can avoid this happening again."

"I hear what you're saying, but it seems like you're justifying your actions, instead of taking responsibility for what you did."

"I understand that apologies are hard, but I also need to feel confident that you understand the impact."

"I appreciate the apology, but I'd also appreciate more clarity on how we're going to move forward from this."

How to Apologise Sincerely and Effectively

Apologising is not just about saying "sorry"; it is about owning your mistake and showing genuine regret. The goal is to make the other person feel heard and understood, not to justify your actions. Avoid making excuses or shifting blame, as these can make your apology seem insincere.

WHAT NOT TO SAY:

"I'm sorry if you felt hurt, but that's not what I meant."
WHY IT SHOULD NOT BE SAID: This makes the apology conditional. It suggests that the other person's feelings might not be valid, and you're only sorry if they misunderstood.

"I didn't do anything wrong, but if you're upset, I guess I'll apologise."
WHY IT SHOULD NOT BE SAID: This shifts the blame to the other person, implying that their feelings are the problem, not your actions.

"I'm sorry, but you also overreacted."
WHY IT SHOULD NOT BE SAID: Adding "but" negates the apology, turning it into an attack or criticism of the other person's reaction.

WHAT TO SAY INSTEAD:

"I want to sincerely apologise for how I acted earlier. I realise now that it wasn't fair to you."

"I'm sorry for any hurt I caused. I should've handled things better, and I'm taking responsibility for that."

"I know I messed up, and I truly regret it. Please let me know how I can make it right."

"I didn't mean to make you feel like that, and I'm sorry if my actions hurt you. Can we talk about how I can improve?"

"I recognise that I was wrong, and I'm committed to learning from this. I hope you can forgive me."

Dealing with People Who Play the Victim

Some people tend to shift the blame onto others or frame themselves as victims to avoid accountability. In both romantic and professional settings, it is important to address this behaviour without feeding into their narrative or invalidating their feelings.

WHAT NOT TO SAY:

"You're always making everything about yourself."
WHY IT SHOULD NOT BE SAID: This escalates the conversation and puts the person on the defensive, which can entrench their victim mentality.

"Stop playing the victim!"
WHY IT SHOULD NOT BE SAID: This phrase is too direct and accusatory, which may only push them deeper into the victim role.

"Fine, I guess I'm the bad guy here."
WHY IT SHOULD NOT BE SAID: This sarcastic response minimises the conversation and shuts down any chance of productive dialogue.

WHAT TO SAY INSTEAD:

"I understand that this is difficult for you, but we need to focus on finding a solution together."

"I hear your concerns, but we both need to take responsibility for our actions."

"I see how you're feeling, but I also want to make sure we're not shifting away from the issue at hand."

"I'm happy to discuss how you're feeling, but I also think it's important to talk about the role we both played."

"I understand that you're upset, but we need to focus on how we can address the situation moving forward."

How to Respond to Gaslighting

Gaslighting is a manipulation tactic where someone tries to make you doubt your perception of reality. Responding to gaslighting requires calmly standing your ground without engaging in a back-and-forth about the validity of your feelings or experiences.

WHAT NOT TO SAY:

"Maybe I'm just overreacting..."
WHY IT SHOULD NOT BE SAID: This undermines your own reality and gives the other person control over the narrative.

"I don't know, maybe you're right."
WHY IT SHOULD NOT BE SAID: This gives the gaslighter power by allowing them to dictate your perception of events.

"You're lying! That's not what happened at all!"
WHY IT SHOULD NOT BE SAID: Accusations, even if accurate, can lead to further manipulation or escalation.

WHAT TO SAY INSTEAD:

"I know what I experienced, and I'm confident in my perspective."

"It feels like we're seeing things differently, but I stand by how I remember it."

"I trust my own judgement and how the situation unfolded."

"We seem to remember this differently, but that doesn't change how I felt in the moment."

"I'm open to discussing this, but I'm also sure of what happened."

How to Respond When They Say You're Being Too Sensitive

Being told that you are "too sensitive" can feel dismissive, as though your emotions are invalid. It is essential to assert the validity of your feelings without allowing the other person to deflect the conversation away from their behaviour.

WHAT NOT TO SAY:

"Maybe I am being too sensitive..."
WHY IT SHOULD NOT BE SAID: This allows the other person to dismiss your emotions and shifts the focus away from the issue at hand.

"You just don't understand me at all!"
WHY IT SHOULD NOT BE SAID: This is overly dramatic and may make the other person feel like they are being unfairly blamed.

"Why do you always say that?!"
WHY IT SHOULD NOT BE SAID: This shifts the conversation from the issue to the frequency of their comments, which can derail the conversation.

WHAT TO SAY INSTEAD:

"My emotions are valid, and I'd like to be heard without being labelled as sensitive."

"I'm not overly sensitive, I only have a brain that notices patterns."

"It's important to me that my feelings are taken seriously, regardless of how you perceive them."

"I understand that you might not feel the same way, but my emotions are still real."

"This is how I feel, and I'd appreciate it if we could address the situation rather than my reaction."

"We can disagree on how to handle this, but my feelings aren't something to dismiss."

Responding to Overly Defensive Behaviour

When someone becomes overly defensive, it can be challenging to continue the conversation without it escalating into an argument. The key is to remain calm and avoid triggering more defensiveness while still addressing the issue.

WHAT NOT TO SAY:

"You're getting so defensive!"
WHY IT SHOULD NOT BE SAID: Pointing out someone's defensiveness only makes them more defensive and shifts the focus from the actual issue.

"Why are you so worked up about this?"
WHY IT SHOULD NOT BE SAID: This question comes across as condescending and makes the other person feel like their reaction is unjustified.

"Calm down, it's not that serious."
WHY IT SHOULD NOT BE SAID: Telling someone to calm down can make them feel like their feelings are being dismissed, intensifying their defensiveness.

WHAT TO SAY INSTEAD:

"I understand this is hard to talk about, but I'm here to work through it with you."

"It feels like this conversation is getting tense. Let's take a step back and try to focus on finding a solution."

"I'm not here to criticise, just to talk about how we can resolve this."

"I see that this is difficult to discuss, but I want to understand where you're coming from."

"Let's both take a moment to breathe. I want to have a constructive conversation without things getting heated."

How to Respond to Fake Compliments

When someone gives a fake compliment, it can be uncomfortable because it often feels insincere or patronising. Here are five advanced ways to handle such moments in a graceful but firm manner.

1. Sometimes, the best way to handle a fake compliment is to acknowledge it, then shift the focus elsewhere.

   WHAT TO SAY:

   "Thanks, I guess you're trying something new with your comments too. So, what's the plan for the day?"

   WHY IT WORKS:

   You acknowledge their attempt without feeding into the insincerity and immediately change the subject, keeping things light but steering the conversation away from their false praise.

2. If the compliment feels a bit too backhanded, you can call it out in a subtle, non-confrontational way.

   WHAT TO SAY:

   "Hmm, I'm not sure if that's a compliment, but I'll take it with a pinch of salt. You know me!"

   WHY IT WORKS:

   It shows that you're aware of the disingenuous tone, but you are not letting it bother you. You maintain control of the conversation with

3. Instead of dwelling on the fake compliment, you can confidently shift the narrative to something positive about yourself, reminding them that you don't need validation.

   WHAT TO SAY:

   "Oh, I wasn't really aiming to impress, but I'm feeling good today. How's your day going?"

   WHY IT WORKS:

   It shows that their insincerity does not affect your confidence. You subtly remind them that you are comfortable with yourself and do not need their approval.

4. Sometimes, humour can be an effective way to defuse a fake compliment, especially if you are in a light-hearted conversation.

   WHAT TO SAY:

   "Ah, I see you're taking notes from the shade academy today. But no worries, I'm still winning."

WHY IT WORKS:

This approach uses sarcasm to let them know you have caught on, but it does not escalate the situation. It allows you to maintain control while keeping the mood light.

5. If the situation allows for it, you can directly question the sincerity of their compliment in a way that does not create tension but subtly calls them out.

WHAT TO SAY:

"Are you sure that's a compliment? It's sounding a little off, but I'll let it slide this time."

WHY IT WORKS:

This challenges the person without being too confrontational. It gives them a chance to correct themselves or at least reflect on what they said, while you remain composed and assertive.

How to Assert Your Needs Without Feeling Guilty

When it comes to asserting your needs, it is common to feel uncomfortable, especially if you are worried about seeming selfish or demanding. Whether it is in a romantic relationship or a professional setting, knowing how to express your needs clearly and respectfully is key to maintaining balance and avoiding resentment. The goal is not to shy away from what you need but to communicate it confidently without feeling guilty.

WHAT *NOT* TO SAY:

"I am sorry to bother you, but could you help me?"

WHY NOT: Apologising makes your need seem like a burden and diminishes its importance.

"It is probably nothing, but I was hoping you could do this for me..."

WHY NOT: Downplaying your need weakens your position and invites dismissal.

"Never mind, it is not that important."

Why not: Backtracking signals that you do not value your own need, making it easier for others to ignore.

What to say:

"I have noticed I am handling a lot of extra tasks lately, and I would appreciate it if we could balance the workload more evenly."

- ✓ Clear and assertive without being demanding.

"I need more support with this project. Can we come up with a solution that works for both of us?"

- ✓ Invites collaboration while affirming your need for support.

"It is important to me that we communicate more regularly about these issues."

- ✓ States your need clearly and highlights its importance to you.

"I feel overwhelmed by the workload and would appreciate your assistance."

- ✓ Acknowledges your feelings and directly requests help.

"To ensure we both succeed, I need X to happen. Can we discuss how to make this work?"

- ✓ Frames your need as beneficial to both parties, and it encourages a positive response.

Responding to Unsolicited Advice

Everyone has experienced the frustration of receiving advice they did not ask for. It could be a colleague, friend, or even a family member who is constantly offering suggestions, whether or not you need them. Responding tactfully while maintaining boundaries is crucial, as you do not want to come off as dismissive or rude, but you also want to stay true to your choices.

What *not* to say:

"Oh, maybe you are right, I should consider that."

WHY NOT: If the advice does not align with your thinking, agreeing just to please them is counterproductive.

"I do not think you know what you are talking about."

WHY NOT: Being blunt can lead to unnecessary conflict, even if you do not value their advice.

"I have been doing this my whole life, I do not need your advice."

WHY NOT: This defensive approach shuts down communication and may come off as arrogant.

WHAT TO SAY:

"Thanks for the suggestion, but I am comfortable with my current approach."

   ✓   Polite but firm, letting them know you have your own plan.

"I appreciate your concern, but I have got this under control."

   ✓   Acknowledges their intent but asserts your independence.

"I will think about it, but for now, I am sticking with what works for me."

   ✓   Shows openness without agreeing to take the advice.

"That is an interesting point, but I see things a bit differently."

   ✓   You are respectful but maintain your stance.

"I understand where you are coming from, but I feel confident in my own decision."

   ✓   Balances respect with self-assurance.

Dealing with People Who Dismiss Your Feelings

It can be deeply frustrating and invalidating when someone dismisses your feelings, whether in a personal or professional relationship. It is important to assert yourself while remaining calm, as responding aggressively might escalate the situation. The key is to acknowledge your emotions and

reinforce their importance, even if the other person does not understand them.

What *not* to say:

"Maybe I am overreacting, but..."

Why not: This immediately undermines your feelings and gives the other person room to dismiss them.

"You are right, I am just being too sensitive."

Why not: Agreeing with their dismissal invalidates your emotional experience.

"Forget it, it is not a big deal."

Why not: Dismissing your own feelings prevents you from addressing the real issue and creates future problems.

What to say:

"I hear what you are saying, but this is how I feel, and I need you to understand that."

- ✓ Asserts your feelings calmly without dismissing theirs.

"It might not seem serious to you, but it is important to me, and I would like us to talk about it."

- ✓ Encourages dialogue while highlighting the importance of your feelings.

"I need you to acknowledge that my feelings are valid, even if you do not agree."

- ✓ Reinforces the need for respect, even in disagreement.

"I understand your perspective, but I would appreciate it if you could see things from my point of view too."

- ✓ Encourages empathy while remaining assertive.

"I know this might not make sense to you, but I am feeling hurt, and I would like us to address that."

✓ Opens up space for a conversation while clearly expressing your hurt.

Dealing with Someone Who Always Wants to Be Right

Dealing with someone who always insists on being right can be exhausting. Whether in a romantic relationship or a professional setting, it often feels like their need to "win" the conversation overshadows the goal of resolving issues or finding common ground. Learning how to handle this without escalating the situation requires patience and careful communication.

WHAT *NOT* TO SAY:

"Fine, you are right. I give up."

WHY NOT: This response is passive-aggressive and does not solve the underlying issue. It only reinforces their behaviour.

"Why do you always have to be right?!"

WHY NOT: This escalates the conflict and shifts the focus to blame instead of resolving the issue.

"You do not know what you are talking about."

WHY NOT: This is dismissive and can make the person defensive, leading to more friction.

WHAT TO SAY:

"I see your point, but I think we should also consider this perspective."

✓ You acknowledge their opinion while introducing your own without directly challenging their need to be right.

"I understand your reasoning, but I have a different view on this."

✓ Calmly asserting that differing opinions are valid.

"We might not agree, but I think it is important we both feel heard."

✓ This shifts the focus from winning to mutual respect.

"Let us agree to disagree on this one, and focus on what we can both work towards."

- ✓ Helps to move past the argument without forcing resolution.

"I appreciate your perspective, but this is how I see it based on my experiences."

- ✓ You validate their viewpoint but also stand your ground.

How to Avoid Taking Things Personally in Arguments

It is easy to get defensive or hurt during an argument, especially when emotions are running high. Whether it is with a partner or a colleague, not taking things personally helps you stay calm and focus on resolving the issue instead of getting caught up in your own emotions. Remember, arguments are often about differing perspectives, not personal attacks.

WHAT *NOT* TO SAY:

"You are always attacking me!"

WHY NOT: This shifts the focus to feeling victimised instead of addressing the actual issue.

"I knew you never really cared about me."

WHY NOT: Jumping to conclusions based on emotions escalates the argument and deepens hurt.

"Why are you making this all about me?"

WHY NOT: This makes the conversation about your feelings rather than addressing the situation.

WHAT TO SAY:

"I know this is a heated conversation, but I do not want to take it personally."

- ✓ This acknowledges the tension while creating a boundary to protect your emotions.

"Let us focus on the issue and not turn this into a personal attack."

✓ Shifts the conversation back to the real problem without emotional overreaction.

"I understand you are frustrated, but let us not make this about us as individuals."

✓ Keeps the focus on resolving the issue and not on personal flaws.

"I want to make sure we are talking about the problem, not each other."

✓ Reinforces the need to stay solution-focused.

"I am trying not to take things personally, so can we approach this calmly?"

✓ Diffuses the situation by acknowledging emotions while asking for a more constructive approach.

How to Stop Apologising Excessively in Conversations

Many people apologise excessively, often out of habit, to avoid conflict or out of a sense of guilt for things that are not their fault. Whether in relationships or professional environments, constantly apologising can undermine your confidence and make others question your assertiveness. It is important to break the habit of unnecessary apologies to maintain your self-respect and communication clarity.

WHAT *NOT* TO SAY:

"I am sorry for interrupting, but..."

WHY NOT: Apologising before speaking minimises the value of your input.

"I am sorry, but could you repeat that?"

WHY NOT: Asking for clarification does not require an apology; you have the right to fully understand.

"Sorry, I did not mean to ask for help."

WHY NOT: This makes it seem like asking for help is a burden, which it is not.

WHAT TO SAY:

"Thank you for your patience while I gather my thoughts."

- ✓ Replaces unnecessary apologies with gratitude and confidence.

"I appreciate you taking the time to explain that again."

- ✓ Shows appreciation without apologising unnecessarily.

"Could you clarify that for me, please?"

- ✓ Directly asks for what you need without undermining yourself.

"I would like to share my thoughts on this as well."

- ✓ Assertively contributes to the conversation without feeling the need to apologise.

"Thanks for bearing with me while I finish this."

- ✓ Reinforces appreciation and avoids apologising for taking your time.

How to Respond to Public Criticism

Public criticism can be uncomfortable and embarrassing, especially if it happens in front of others. Whether it is in a work meeting, a social gathering, or on social media, how you respond can determine how the situation unfolds. It is important to handle the criticism with grace and tact, allowing you to maintain your composure and credibility.

WHAT *NOT* TO SAY:

"Well, that is just your opinion!"

WHY NOT: This defensive response dismisses the critique without addressing its substance and can make you seem combative.

"You do not know what you are talking about."

Why not: This can escalate the situation and create unnecessary conflict in a public setting.

"I cannot believe you would say that in front of everyone!"

Why not: Expressing shock or hurt publicly can make the situation more dramatic and escalate tension.

What to say:

"Thank you for your feedback, I will take that into consideration."

- ✓ A gracious and calm response that shows you are open to improvement.

"I understand your point, and I will work on that moving forward."

- ✓ Acknowledges the criticism without feeling the need to argue.

"I appreciate the insight, and I will reflect on how to address it."

- ✓ Keeps the tone positive and professional, showing willingness to grow.

"I hear your concerns, and I will make sure to address them appropriately."

- ✓ Shows that you are listening and are prepared to take action.

"Thank you for bringing that to my attention, let us discuss how to move forward."

- ✓ A constructive approach that shifts the conversation toward resolution rather than lingering on the criticism.

How to Respond to Gaslighting

Gaslighting is a subtle but powerful form of manipulation that can make you doubt your reality. Whether in a relationship or a professional setting, it is important to recognise when someone is trying to twist the truth and make you question your memory, feelings, or perceptions. Dealing with gaslighting is not easy, but knowing how to respond can help you regain

control of the situation and stand your ground without second-guessing yourself.

WHAT TO SAY:

"I remember things differently, and I would like to stick to the facts."

- ✓ This statement asserts your memory and shows that you are not willing to let them distort the truth.

"I feel like we are talking in circles, let us focus on resolving the issue rather than questioning what happened."

- ✓ Helps shift the conversation from denial or manipulation to problem-solving.

"I understand that you have a different perspective, but that does not invalidate how I am feeling."

- ✓ Acknowledges their point of view without letting it overshadow your reality.

"Let us agree to focus on what we can change instead of debating the past."

- ✓ This encourages moving forward rather than being stuck in distorted arguments.

"I am not comfortable with how this conversation is making me doubt myself."

- ✓ Directly calls out the manipulative behaviour and sets a boundary.

WHAT NOT TO SAY:

"Maybe you are right, and I am overreacting."

WHY NOT: This gives in to their narrative and weakens your position.

"I guess I did not remember correctly after all."

WHY NOT: It allows them to control the narrative, making you question your own recollection.

"It must have been my fault if you are saying it that way."

WHY NOT: This kind of response plays into their manipulation, making you feel guilty for something that may not be true.

How to Address Sarcasm Without Being Defensive

Sarcasm can often be a mask for passive aggression, and it is easy to feel attacked when someone makes a snide remark. However, responding with defensiveness can escalate the situation, turning it into a bigger issue than it needs to be. Instead, knowing how to address sarcasm calmly and directly can help you keep your cool while still calling out the inappropriate behaviour.

WHAT TO SAY:

"That sounded a bit sarcastic. Could you clarify what you really mean?"

- ✓ This response highlights the sarcasm without escalating the situation, inviting the other person to be direct.

"I am not sure I understood your tone. Can you explain that in a different way?"

- ✓ By asking for clarification, you give them a chance to drop the sarcasm and have a genuine conversation.

"I would appreciate it if we could talk about this without the jokes, I want to understand your point."

- ✓ Directly asking for a more serious approach shows you are not here for games.

"I think this conversation would be more productive if we stayed clear and straightforward."

- ✓ Encourages constructive dialogue and subtly calls out their sarcasm.

"I am sensing some tension behind that comment, can we address that directly?"

- ✓ This approach acknowledges the underlying emotion and redirects the conversation to the real issue.

"Why are you always so sarcastic with me?"

WHY NOT: This can sound accusatory and make the person even more defensive or sarcastic.

"Do you think that was funny?"

WHY NOT: It turns the conversation into a confrontation and invites more passive-aggressive responses.

"I know you did not mean that, but it still hurts."

WHY NOT: This makes it seem like you are brushing it off, but still letting it affect you, which can give them more reason to continue being sarcastic.

How to Manage Conflicts with Manipulative People

Conflicts with manipulative people are some of the most challenging. They often twist words, shift blame, and use emotional tactics to make you feel at fault or confused. Navigating these situations requires a strong sense of self-awareness and the ability to set firm boundaries, all while remaining calm and clear-headed. The goal is not to win the argument but to avoid getting caught in their web of manipulation.

WHAT TO SAY:

"I am noticing that this conversation is going in circles. Let us focus on finding a solution."

- ✓ Stops the manipulation from continuing by focusing on resolution.

"I will not accept being blamed for something I did not do. Let us stick to the facts."

- ✓ Sets a firm boundary and refuses to take the bait of shifting blame.

"I feel like we are not addressing the real issue. Let us talk about what is really bothering you."

- ✓ Calls out any misdirection and brings the conversation back to the core problem.

"I am not comfortable with how this is being handled. Can we take a break and come back to it when we are both calm?"

- ✓ This response pauses the manipulation and creates space for a more balanced discussion.

"I am not okay with how this conversation is going. I think it is best to step away for now."

- ✓ Removes yourself from the situation before the manipulation can escalate further.

WHAT NOT TO SAY:

"I do not understand why you are acting like this."

WHY NOT: This gives them an opportunity to manipulate the narrative further and paint themselves as the victim.

"I guess you are right, I was wrong."

WHY NOT: This validates their manipulative tactics and weakens your position in future conversations.

"Fine, let us just drop it then."

WHY NOT: Ignoring the manipulation does not solve the issue and allows it to continue unchecked in future interactions.

Recognising When to Walk Away from a Conflict

Knowing when to walk away from a conflict is a vital skill, whether you are dealing with your partner or your colleague. Some arguments simply cannot be resolved in the heat of the moment, and staying can do more harm than good. Walking away does not mean you are giving up; it means you are prioritising your peace and choosing not to engage in a fruitless exchange. It is about protecting your mental and emotional well-being.

WHAT TO SAY:

"I feel like this conversation is not going anywhere. Let us take a break and revisit it later."

- ✓ This calmly signals that continuing the argument will not be productive and suggests returning to it when emotions have settled.

"I need some time to cool off before we continue. Can we talk about this again when we are both in a better headspace?"

- ✓ Taking a pause gives both parties the opportunity to reflect and approach the issue more constructively.

"I am not ready to talk about this right now. Let us come back to it when we can have a more respectful conversation."

- ✓ This sets a boundary and prevents the argument from spiralling into something more harmful.

"I do not think we are going to resolve this right now. Let us agree to step away and talk about it later."

- ✓ By suggesting stepping away, you avoid unnecessary conflict and allow time for perspective.

"I can tell this conversation is getting heated. I think it is best to stop here and continue when we are both calm."

- ✓ Acknowledges the rising tension and takes responsibility for creating a more positive space for discussion.

WHAT NOT TO SAY:

"You are impossible to talk to, I am done."

WHY NOT: This statement escalates the situation and leaves the conflict unresolved, creating lingering resentment.

"Fine, walk away, you never want to solve anything."

WHY NOT: This guilt-tripping response keeps the argument going instead of promoting a healthy break.

"Whatever, I do not care anymore."

WHY NOT: This dismissive attitude shows you are avoiding the issue rather than addressing it later, making the problem worse in the long run.

How to Respond When Somebody Tells a Lie

When someone lies to you, it can be frustrating, hurtful, and even shocking, especially if it is a person you trust. Responding to lies effectively requires a calm approach, as reacting impulsively or aggressively can escalate the situation. The aim is to address the lie directly yet calmly, making it clear that honesty is valued in the relationship, whether personal or professional. Here's how to handle this delicate situation, along with things to avoid saying.

WHAT TO SAY:

"I want to clarify something because it seems like there is a misunderstanding. Can you go over this with me again?"

- ✓ This approach is gentle yet probing, allowing the person a chance to correct themselves without feeling attacked.

"I have a different understanding of the situation, and I think it is important to be on the same page. Could you explain your side?"

- ✓ This opens a dialogue and shows that you are interested in the truth without making direct accusations.

"I value honesty in our relationship, so it concerns me when things do not seem to match up. Can we talk about what happened?"

- ✓ This makes it clear that honesty is important to you while giving the other person a chance to clarify.

"From what I know, it seems like there is a discrepancy here. Could we go over it together to understand each other better?"

- ✓ This suggests collaboration in finding the truth rather than confrontation, keeping the tone open and respectful.

"I think we should clear this up to avoid any future misunderstandings. Can we be straightforward about what really happened?"

- ✓ This directly calls for honesty and transparency while maintaining a calm, solution-oriented approach.

"I know you are lying, so just admit it already."

WHY NOT: Accusing someone outright often leads to defensiveness or further lies, which can quickly escalate the conflict.

"I cannot believe you would lie to me like that. Do you think I am stupid?"

WHY NOT: This approach comes off as accusatory and may turn the conversation into a confrontation rather than a constructive discussion.

"You always lie about everything. Why should I trust you now?"

WHY NOT: Bringing up past issues or generalising the situation creates defensiveness and may prevent any resolution in the current situation.

How to Avoid Overthinking Conflict Situations

Overthinking conflicts can make things seem worse than they actually are. You may find yourself replaying situations in your mind, imagining how things could have been different, or second-guessing your actions and responses. While it is natural to reflect on conflicts, getting stuck in a loop of "what ifs" and "should haves" can intensify stress. Here is how to approach conflicts without overthinking and how to avoid common pitfalls in the process.

WHAT TO SAY:

"I am acknowledging the issue and choosing to focus on what I can actually control."

- ✓ This helps remind yourself to stay grounded and not dwell on things outside your influence.

"I have reflected on my role in this, and I am now ready to let it go and move forward."

- ✓ This statement shows that you are moving from reflection to action, which reduces endless analysis.

"I need to put things in perspective. This one conflict does not define me or the relationship."

✓ Perspective helps reduce overthinking by focusing on the bigger picture rather than getting lost in details.

"I am choosing to give myself grace. It is okay that things were not perfect, and I am learning from it."

✓ Acknowledging imperfections allows you to accept what happened without endless rumination.

"Let me focus on a positive step I can take instead of worrying about everything that might go wrong."

✓ By choosing one constructive action, you move forward instead of being trapped in hypothetical concerns.

WHAT NOT TO SAY:

"I have to replay every detail to figure out what went wrong."

WHY NOT: This habit intensifies overthinking and makes it harder to reach a sense of closure.

"If only I had done that differently, none of this would have happened."

WHY NOT: Thinking in terms of "if only" keeps you trapped in regret and focuses on the past rather than the future.

"I cannot let this go until I have analysed every angle."

WHY NOT: Overanalyzing rarely leads to resolution; instead, it heightens stress and anxiety about the situation.

Recognizing and Avoiding Emotional Triggers

Emotional triggers are reactions tied to past experiences, sensitive topics, or unresolved issues, often intensifying emotions in ways that seem out of proportion. Learning to identify and manage these triggers can help you respond thoughtfully in the moment rather than reacting impulsively. Here are ways to approach emotional triggers constructively, and a few phrases to avoid that can make situations worse.

WHAT TO SAY:

"I noticed that this situation stirred up strong feelings for me. Let me take a moment to breathe."

 ✓ Pausing to reflect helps you calm down before responding, which reduces reactionary responses.

"This reminds me of a past experience, so I want to ensure I am not reacting based on old feelings."

 ✓ This self-awareness encourages you to differentiate between past and present, reducing the intensity of the trigger.

"I feel that my reaction might be heightened, so let me take some time to process before I respond."

 ✓ Giving yourself time to process helps prevent impulsive responses that may not be constructive.

"I am recognizing my emotions and making sure I respond based on what is happening now."

 ✓ Focusing on the present situation helps you respond in a way that is more grounded and measured.

"Let me step back and check in with myself before I continue the conversation."

 ✓ Taking a break can prevent you from reacting to the trigger, allowing you to handle the conversation calmly.

WHAT NOT TO SAY:

"I cannot believe you just said that!"

WHY NOT: This is often a reaction to a trigger that escalates conflict without fully understanding the situation.

"You are just like everyone else who has hurt me."

WHY NOT: This statement brings in past experiences and can feel unfair to the other person, often intensifying the issue.

"I am done. I cannot handle this."

WHY NOT: Shutting down can end the conversation without resolution and can leave emotions unresolved, worsening the trigger.

How to Handle Emotional Blackmail in Relationships

Emotional blackmail is a form of manipulation where someone uses guilt, fear, or obligation to control your actions. Recognising this behaviour is key to responding effectively without giving in or escalating the situation. Here are some ways to respond, as well as things to avoid saying that could make the situation more difficult.

WHAT TO SAY:

"I understand that you feel strongly about this, but I need to make this decision for myself."

- ✓ By acknowledging their emotions, you remain compassionate while setting a boundary.

"I would like us to communicate openly without resorting to guilt or pressure."

- ✓ This statement directly addresses the behaviour without being confrontational.

"I value our relationship, but I also need to feel respected in my decisions."

- ✓ Expressing the importance of respect reinforces the value of healthy boundaries.

"It seems like we have different perspectives here. Let us find a way to discuss this without imposing on each other."

- ✓ Emphasising mutual respect encourages a balanced discussion instead of control.

"Let us agree to speak honestly and allow each other the freedom to make our own choices."

- ✓ Highlighting honesty and independence supports a healthier, guilt-free exchange.

WHAT NOT TO SAY:

"Fine, have it your way if it means that much to you."

WHY NOT: This statement concedes to manipulation and may encourage more emotional blackmail in the future.

"I guess I am just a terrible person for not doing what you want."

WHY NOT: Responding with sarcasm intensifies guilt and reinforces the manipulative behaviour.

"You are just trying to make me feel guilty, and it is not going to work."

WHY NOT: This can escalate the situation by adding defensiveness and hostility.

How to Stop Stonewalling in Arguments

Stonewalling, or shutting down during arguments, can create distance and unresolved issues in relationships. While it may seem like an easy way to avoid conflict, it often leaves the other person feeling ignored or dismissed. Here is how to address your feelings without resorting to stonewalling, along with statements to avoid that may escalate tension.

WHAT TO SAY:

"I need a few moments to gather my thoughts so I can discuss this calmly."

- ✓ This explains your need for space without making the other person feel shut out.

"I am feeling overwhelmed right now. Can we take a break and revisit this soon?"

- ✓ Taking a break helps manage emotions without ending the conversation altogether.

"I am committed to resolving this, but I need to take a moment to reflect first."

✓ Showing commitment to resolution while acknowledging your feelings helps maintain connection.

"I do not want to shut down, so I am taking a moment to process everything."

✓ This openly communicates your intention to engage, even if you need a short break.

"Let us pause for a moment so that we can return to this with a clear mind."

✓ A pause allows you to regroup and come back to the discussion with a clearer perspective.

WHAT NOT TO SAY:

"I am done talking about this."

WHY NOT: This shuts down the conversation completely, often leaving the other person feeling abandoned or ignored.

"Whatever, think what you want."

WHY NOT: This sounds dismissive and can make the other person feel like their perspective is not valued.

"This conversation is pointless."

WHY NOT: Dismissing the conversation dismisses the other person's feelings, which can escalate the argument rather than resolve it.

How to Disengage from Toxic Conversations

Disengaging from toxic conversations can be a powerful tool for protecting your mental well-being. Toxic conversations are often unproductive, emotionally draining, and can leave you feeling worse than when they started. It is important to know how to set boundaries gracefully and exit the conversation when necessary. Here are effective ways to disengage, and a few things to avoid saying that can make the situation more volatile.

"I appreciate your point of view, but I think it is best we continue this conversation another time."

- ✓ Acknowledges the other person while calmly closing the conversation.

"I feel that this conversation is getting too heated, so I am going to step back for now."

- ✓ This is a direct yet gentle way to state that you are opting out.

"This does not feel constructive, and I prefer not to continue if we are not making progress."

- ✓ Recognizes that the conversation is unproductive without sounding dismissive.

"I am happy to discuss this when we can both be calm and respectful."

- ✓ Offers an opportunity to revisit the topic under better conditions.

"Let us take a break and revisit this when emotions have settled."

- ✓ This helps both parties regroup and refocus.

WHAT NOT TO SAY:

"This is just pointless."

WHY NOT: This phrase invalidates the other person and can escalate anger or frustration.

"You are not making any sense."

WHY NOT: This statement sounds condescending and can make the other person defensive.

"I am done with this nonsense."

WHY NOT: This phrase is likely to provoke further argument rather than ending the conversation peacefully.

How to Keep Your Cool When Provoked

When someone provokes you, staying calm can be challenging but is essential to maintaining self-control and responding effectively. Keeping your cool in these moments helps you to think clearly, avoid saying things you may regret, and often de-escalates the situation. Here are some constructive ways to keep your composure, along with things to avoid saying that may intensify the conflict.

WHAT TO SAY:

"I am choosing to stay calm here and not let this get to me."

- ✓ This empowers you to stay in control and reminds you to focus on your own response.

"I understand you have a strong opinion, and I respect that."

- ✓ Acknowledges their feelings while keeping the conversation civil.

"I am going to take a deep breath before I respond."

- ✓ This gives you a moment to compose yourself, helping to prevent a reactive response.

"Let us take a step back and look at this calmly."

- ✓ Reframes the situation and invites a more level-headed discussion.

"I hear you, and I am processing what you are saying."

- ✓ Validates the other person without agreeing or reacting immediately.

WHAT NOT TO SAY:

"Why are you being so unreasonable?"

WHY NOT: This can make the other person defensive and intensify the situation.

"You are just trying to get a reaction out of me."

WHY NOT: This statement may increase tension by making them feel accused.

"Calm down!"

Why not: Telling someone to "calm down" often has the opposite effect and escalates emotions.

How to Manage Your Tone During Difficult Conversations

Managing your tone in challenging conversations is key to ensuring that your message is received without adding unnecessary tension. Often, what you say is less important than *how* you say it. By keeping a calm, steady tone, you can convey your message clearly while maintaining respect. Here are ways to adjust your tone for better outcomes and phrases to avoid that may come off as harsh or accusatory.

What to say:

"I want us to discuss this openly, and I am going to keep my tone calm to do so."

- ✓ This shows your intent to communicate respectfully and encourages the other person to do the same.

"I am here to listen, and I will make sure to keep my voice steady."

- ✓ Demonstrates self-awareness and helps the other person feel heard.

"I understand this is important, so I will speak in a way that shows my respect for you."

- ✓ Communicates your commitment to a respectful dialogue, even in difficult moments.

"I am making a conscious effort to be clear without raising my voice."

- ✓ Acknowledges your control over your tone and may encourage the other person to mirror it.

"Let us both aim to speak calmly to make sure we understand each other fully."

✓ Sets a collaborative tone, emphasising mutual respect.

WHAT NOT TO SAY:

"Stop taking things so seriously!"

WHY NOT: This sounds dismissive and may make the other person feel belittled.

"You are being overly sensitive about this."

WHY NOT: This statement minimises their feelings, which can escalate the issue.

"It is not a big deal."

WHY NOT: This can come across as indifferent and may prevent a constructive conversation.

How to Navigate Conversations with Overly Emotional People

Interacting with people who become overly emotional during conversations can be challenging, especially when emotions take over the discussion. Understanding how to approach these situations with empathy while maintaining your own boundaries can help you keep the conversation productive. Here are ways to navigate such conversations effectively, as well as a few phrases to avoid.

WHAT TO SAY:

"I see that this is important to you, and I want to hear what you have to say."

✓ This validates their feelings, showing that you value their perspective.

"I understand that this is an emotional topic, and I will do my best to listen patiently."

✓ Reinforces your commitment to staying calm and supportive.

"Let us take things one step at a time so we can both feel comfortable in this conversation."

- ✓ Slows down the conversation, making it easier to process emotions.

"I can see this has brought up strong feelings. Take your time."

- ✓ Provides reassurance, encouraging them to express themselves without feeling rushed.

"I want us both to feel heard and understood, so let us focus on finding some common ground."

- ✓ Emphasises mutual respect and encourages a more balanced exchange.

WHAT NOT TO SAY:

"You are overreacting."

WHY NOT: This dismisses their emotions and can make the person feel misunderstood.

"Why are you getting so worked up about this?"

WHY NOT: This can sound judgmental and may lead to an even more emotional response.

"Can you calm down so we can talk like adults?"

WHY NOT: This is likely to offend, as it implies they are not handling themselves maturely.

CHAPTER 3

COMMUNICATION AND SOCIAL SKILLS

Often, we find ourselves in settings where we want to connect with others—whether at a networking event, a social gathering, or even a casual meeting—but are unsure how to open a conversation in a way that feels both natural and polished. Here are 30 ways to approach these situations, complete with examples and dialogues to make them truly practical.

1.   Compliment Their Choice of Attire or Accessory

A genuine compliment on something noticeable, like an accessory, can easily warm up a conversation.

Example: "I really like your watch; it is quite unique. Does it have a story behind it?"

2.   Ask About Their Journey to the Event

This is especially relevant if it was a challenging commute or if the event is out of town.

Example: "How was your journey here? I had quite an adventure with traffic, but I am here now!"

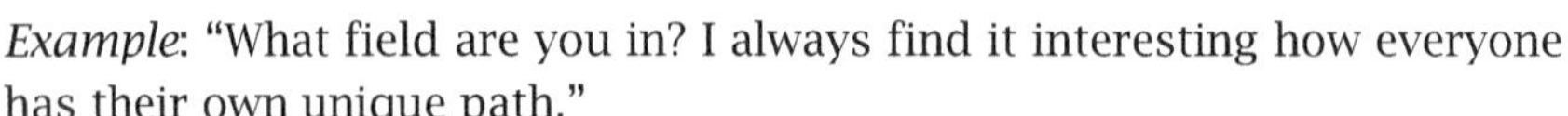

3.   Show Interest in Their Role or Profession

People love to talk about what they do when asked with sincere curiosity.

Example: "What field are you in? I always find it interesting how everyone has their own unique path."

4.   Ask for Their Opinion on a Common Topic

Bringing up a relatable subject helps create an instant connection.

Example: "I noticed the speaker mentioned digital transformation. What do you think about the changes it is bringing to our field?"

5.   Use a Shared Experience as an Entry Point

If you notice someone laughing at a joke or appreciating something around you, it can be a good start.

Example: "I could not help but laugh at that comment too! It is great to meet someone with the same sense of humour."

6.   Ask for Recommendations

Whether it is about a book, a local restaurant, or even something in the room, people love to share what they know.

Example: "I am looking for a good book to read. Do you have any recommendations?"

7.   Bring Up a Current Event (with Caution)

Be mindful of the topic, but some current events are safe and open for discussion.

Example: "Did you hear about the recent tech conference in Lagos? It seems like such a game-changer."

8.   Mention Something Unique About the Venue

If the location has something notable, it can be a good way to get the conversation going.

Example: "This is a stunning venue. Have you attended events here before?"

9.   Ask What Drew Them to the Event

Simple and direct, this question invites the person to share their motivation for attending.

Example: "What brought you here today? It seems like a very interesting event."

10. Show Curiosity About Their Hometown

If you find out where they are from, a little curiosity about their hometown can go a long way.

Example: "You are from Nairobi? I have heard so much about it but have never been. What is one thing you would say a visitor should not miss?"

11. Introduce Yourself and Offer a Brief Background

Sometimes, introducing yourself directly with a bit about who you are can set a welcoming tone.

Example: "Hi, I am Tobi. I work in communication strategy. What is your area of interest?"

12. Express Curiosity About Their Recent Projects

Professionals often have ongoing projects, which can make for exciting conversation.

Example: "Are you working on any interesting projects currently? I always enjoy hearing about people's creative processes."

13. Ask What They Find Most Interesting About the Industry

This is a great conversation starter for networking events.

Example: "What is one trend in our industry that you find most fascinating right now?"

14. Offer a Thoughtful Observation about the Event Atmosphere

Commenting on the vibe can lead to mutual agreement and further discussion.

Example: "The energy here is quite inspiring, is it not? Have you attended similar events before?"

15. Inquire About a Recent Travel Experience

Travel often leads to great stories and insights.

Example: "Have you been on any interesting trips recently? I find travelling gives such a fresh perspective."

16. Mention a Book or Article That Could Be Relevant to Them

This approach shows that you have done your homework and adds value to the conversation.

Example: "I read an article recently about AI in healthcare. It made me think of how it might affect roles like yours. Have you noticed any changes?"

17. Appreciate Their Efforts in the Event if They Are Organisers

Showing appreciation can go a long way.

Example: "I must say, the organisation here is top-notch. Are you part of the planning team?"

18. Ask for Their Insight on a Topic You Are Learning About

If you are genuinely curious, ask them to share their perspective.

Example: "I am trying to understand the impact of fintech on traditional banking. Do you have any thoughts on that?"

19. Ask What They Are Looking Forward to This Year

People enjoy discussing their goals and plans.

Example: "We are almost halfway through the year—what are you most looking forward to achieving?"

20. Use Light Humour to Break the Ice

A little humour can be just the thing to lighten the mood.

Example: "I told myself I would not be the first to reach for a snack, but the food here looks too tempting. Are you a foodie as well?"

21. Talk About Something You Have Recently Learned

Sharing something you learned can prompt them to share their thoughts.

Example: "I just learned about the concept of digital minimalism. It has really got me thinking. Have you heard of it?"

22. Ask About Their Favourite Part of Their Job

Most people have aspects they enjoy most, and they will appreciate your interest.

Example: "What is the favourite part of your job? I always find it fascinating to hear people's passions."

23. Bring Up a Relevant Professional Challenge

This can lead to valuable discussions and even professional advice.

Example: "One of the challenges I face in communication strategy is handling different perspectives. How do you navigate that in your field?"

24. Ask Their Thoughts on a New Development in Your Shared Industry

If there is a new trend, people are likely to have opinions on it.

Example: "With all the AI developments, it feels like our industry is changing every day. What are your thoughts on it?"

25. Express Admiration for an Achievement

Complimenting an accomplishment helps create rapport.

Example: "I heard you completed that project ahead of schedule—that is impressive! How did you manage it?"

26. Share a Fun Fact or Observation Related to the Occasion

This adds an interesting twist to a traditional conversation.

Example: "Did you know this building used to be a theatre? I find it amazing how spaces transform over time."

27. Ask About Their Goals in Attending the Event

This can reveal their interests and make for a smooth conversation.

Example: "What are you hoping to take away from this event? I am looking to expand my network a bit."

28. Mention a Speaker or Topic You Are Eager to Hear About

This builds anticipation and common ground.

Example: "I am particularly excited about the session on emerging markets. Any talks you are looking forward to?"

29. Bring Up a Cultural Reference, Like a Popular Film or Series

Mentioning a well-known series or movie can create an instant bond.

> *Example*: "Have you watched the latest season of that series everyone is talking about? It sparked quite a few debates among my friends."

30. Ask What They Find Most Rewarding in Their Field

A positive approach can lead to an inspiring conversation.

> *Example*: "What is the most rewarding part of your work? I find it fascinating how different fields have their own unique challenges and rewards."

Examples of Starting Conversations in Different Scenarios

NETWORKING EVENT

You: *"I really like your watch; it is quite unique. Does it have a story behind it?"*

James: *"Thank you! Actually, it was a gift from my grandfather. He gave it to me right after I finished my Master's program."*

You: *"That is amazing. A watch with such sentimental value—and it is a classic piece too! Did he wear it for a long time?"*

James: *"Yes, he did. It was actually his favourite. Every time I wear it, I feel connected to him."*

You: *"That is beautiful. So, what field did you study in your Master's?"*

James: *"Business Management, and now I am working in logistics. What about you?"*

CASUAL SOCIAL GATHERING

You: *"Hi, I am Aisha. I work in communication strategy. What is your area of interest?"*

Fatima: *"Nice to meet you, Aisha! I am Fatima. I am in digital marketing."*

You: *"Digital marketing—that must keep you on your toes with all the changes in social media and algorithms!"*

Fatima: *"Absolutely! Every day there is something new to learn. I actually just attended a workshop on it."*

You: *"That is interesting! I have been curious about the latest trends in digital marketing. What was one of the main takeaways from the workshop?"*

BUSINESS CONFERENCE

You: *"The energy here is quite inspiring, is it not? Have you attended similar events before?"*

Amara: *"Yes, I have attended a few conferences, but this one feels more engaging."*

You: *"I agree! The sessions have been really practical. I am especially looking forward to the talk on AI in business. How about you?"*

Amara: *"Same here! I am in data analytics, so AI is quite relevant to my work."*

You: *"That sounds fascinating. Have you already integrated AI into your processes, or is it something you are exploring?"*

Remember, starting a conversation does not have to feel forced; often, all it takes is a little curiosity and a genuine interest in the person in front of you

CHAPTER 4

PUBLIC SPEAKING

In this chapter, we will explore the essential components of effective public speaking, including preparing your speech, organising your ideas, using language effectively, and engaging your audience. We will also discuss practical strategies for managing your nerves, building confidence, and developing your personal style as a speaker. Throughout the chapter, you will find tips and techniques for enhancing your performance, as well as real-world examples of successful speakers who have overcome their own challenges and achieved great success.

Struggling With Stage Fright

Each time I had to speak in front of an audience or in public, I felt nervous, afraid, or anxious, just like you. On top of that, I experienced physical symptoms—sweating, shaking, and my heart racing. There were moments when I just wished the ground would swallow me whole. My mind would fill with negative thoughts, self-doubt, and it became hard to focus.

I want you to know something interesting: many of the speakers and singers you admire so much struggled with stage fright, too.

Now, picture this. I spent most of my school days in the bustling area of Ketu, Lagos. My secondary school had this tradition of holding debates and speeches. I really wanted to be one of the speakers, but there was a huge problem — the excitement of being in the spotlight was just as overwhelming as it was thrilling.

As the debate day crept closer, I became more nervous. My balcony, which used to be a place where I could relax, quickly turned into my practice ground. But no matter how many times I tried, the words just would not come out right. They stayed stuck on paper, refusing to flow naturally

when I spoke. The character I had imagined myself becoming seemed so distant — like it was there, but I just could not reach it. And the more I practised, the more doubts crept in. It was scary.

Even the teachers tried to help, but honestly, it felt like they were using thread to fix something that needed stronger tools. They told me to speak loudly and embody the character, but it all sounded too abstract, too far from what I could understand.

Then, the big day arrived. Stepping onto that stage felt like walking into a bright, glaring spotlight, and all eyes were on me. As soon as I started speaking, the words tangled themselves up, and that character I was supposed to be? Nowhere to be found. The audience, who had just been regular people minutes ago, suddenly became these judgemental figures. I could hear whispers, and even giggles, that felt like a hard punch to my gut. When I finished, the silence in the room was deafening, and the wave of embarrassment hit me hard.

Walking off that stage, my shoulders were heavy, and my heart sank. The harsh reality of losing the battle with stage fright sank in. It was a humbling moment. Despite everything I had done to prepare, the fear on stage was too strong.

But instead of letting that experience break me, I decided to carry it with me. It became a reminder that failing, even though it stings, does not mean it is over. It is just part of the process. That failure was just one chapter, one step towards growing and understanding my limits. Stage fright did not magically disappear, but it stopped being something I was ashamed of. It became a piece of my story — proof of the strength that comes from facing my fears, no matter how vulnerable I felt.

I realised it was time to confront this fear head-on. But first, I had to understand why I felt it in the first place.

Why You Fear Public Speaking

I decided to do some research to understand why I felt this way, and what I found was surprising.

A Fascinating Thought

As humans, we have a natural need to fit in, and we go to great lengths to blend into social groups. This is because we want to belong, and we often try to follow society's rules, even if they do not always align with our personal beliefs. This need to fit in comes from an ancient part of our brain that pushes us to be social creatures.

When you worry about the potential consequences of slipping up a presentation, it is because a part of your brain, the hypothalamus, triggers a chain reaction. It tells your pituitary gland to release a hormone called ACTH, which then tells your adrenal glands, located on top of your kidneys, to release adrenaline. This floods your body with a rush of energy, commonly known as the fight or flight response. Basically, your fear of public speaking is your body's way of trying to protect you.

I found this quite fascinating! The brain keeps reacting with fear until you teach it that there is nothing to be afraid of. Do I sound like a psychologist yet? Maybe a little!

A Deeper Dive

The fact that your brain will continue to react this way until you retrain it is an interesting idea. It shows how our brains are wired to respond to fear, even if it is not always necessary.

Our brains evolved to help us survive. Back in the day, when our ancestors faced real dangers, like wild animals, the brain's fear response was crucial for staying alive. However, in today's world, many of those dangers no longer exist. But the brain still reacts in the same way. So, even though giving a speech in front of an audience is not life-threatening, your brain might still react with fear as if it is.

To stop this automatic response, you need to slowly teach your brain that there is no real danger. This happens through exposure—by repeatedly facing the situation in a safe and controlled way, your brain learns that it is okay. Over time, this helps rewire your brain, and the fear starts to fade.

This is actually how many psychological therapies work. For example, in exposure therapy, people are safely exposed to the things they fear,

helping their brain adjust and reduce the fear over time. In public speaking, as you practise and nothing bad happens, your brain starts to understand that there is no need to be afraid.

The Role of the Hypothalamus

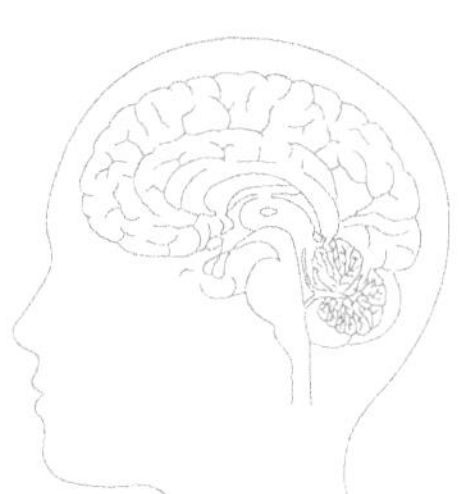

The hypothalamus is a small part of your brain that plays a big role in the body's response to stress, especially when it comes to public speaking. Here is how it works:

1. THE STRESS REACTION STARTS
   When you feel nervous about speaking in front of people, your amygdala (the emotional centre of the brain) sends a signal to your hypothalamus, which starts the stress response.

2. RELEASE OF STRESS HORMONES
   The hypothalamus then triggers the release of stress hormones, mainly cortisol and adrenaline. These hormones get your body ready for a "fight or flight" response.

3. PHYSICAL CHANGES
   Once these hormones are released, you notice changes in your body—your heart rate increases, you breathe faster, your blood pressure rises, and you become more alert. Your body is preparing for what it thinks is a threat.

4. HEIGHTENED AWARENESS
   Because of the stress hormones, you become more aware of your surroundings, like how the audience is reacting. This can make you even more anxious.

5. EFFECT ON THINKING
   These hormones also affect how you think. You might find it hard to concentrate, your mind might race, and it might be difficult to remember what you planned to say.

6. EMOTIONAL IMPACT
   Finally, this process increases your feelings of fear and anxiety, which makes the whole experience of public speaking more stressful.

I hope this helps you understand why you feel the way you do when speaking in public, and why it is not entirely in your control—at least, not yet. With practice and time, you can retrain your brain to react differently. It is all about teaching it that there is no real danger and that you are completely safe.

What You Are Doing Wrong

Realising where there are loopholes is one step toward success. Interestingly, many of the most famous people that are in the public eye and on stage had a fear of speaking in front of people. For example, Oprah Winfrey, known for her powerful and engaging communication skills, has talked about feeling nervous before important speaking engagements. She has mentioned that she still gets butterflies before going on stage, even after years of experience.

In the early 1980s, Oprah was offered the opportunity to co-host a local Baltimore talk show called "People Are Talking." This was a big break for her, but it also came with immense pressure and nervousness. Oprah had never hosted a television show before, and the thought of speaking in front of a live audience was incredibly daunting for her.

As the day of her first show approached, Oprah's anxiety grew. She couldn't sleep the night before, and on the day of the show, her heart raced with anticipation. She felt the weight of the responsibility and the eyes of the audience upon her.

Backstage, Oprah took a moment to centre herself. She closed her eyes, took deep breaths, and reminded herself of her purpose: to connect with her audience and provide a platform for meaningful conversations. She focused on the potential impact her show could have on people's lives.

When the time came for her to step onto the stage, Oprah felt a mixture of fear and determination. She knew she had to push through her stage fright and give it her all. As she began speaking, Oprah gradually found her rhythm. She spoke from the heart, engaging with her guests and the audience with authenticity and warmth.

As the show progressed, Oprah's confidence grew. She realised that she was capable of not only speaking in front of an audience but also creating

a meaningful and impactful experience for her viewers. By the end of the episode, Oprah had not only overcome her stage fright but had also delivered a successful and engaging show.

This experience marked a turning point in Oprah's career. It taught her the power of preparation, self-belief, and the importance of connecting with her audience on a genuine level. From that moment on, Oprah continued to refine her skills as a communicator and host, ultimately becoming one of the most influential and beloved media personalities of our time. Her ability to conquer her stage fright and connect with audiences is a testament to her resilience, determination, and unwavering commitment to making a positive impact through her platform.

Avoid These Pitfalls When Addressing Your Audience

1. Lack of Preparation

Inadequate preparation not only results in a disorganised presentation but also leaves the speaker vulnerable to stumbling, forgetting key points, and appearing unprofessional. It reflects a lack of commitment to delivering a polished and impactful message.

2. Poor Body Language

Beyond conveying disinterest, poor body language includes fidgeting, lack of facial expression, and an overall lack of dynamism. Such non-verbal cues can make the audience feel disconnected and contribute to a negative perception of the speaker's confidence and authenticity.

3. Speaking Too Quickly

Rapid speech not only compromises clarity but also inhibits the speaker's ability to modulate their voice effectively. This lack of variation makes it difficult for the audience to discern the speaker's emphasis on critical points and detracts from the overall persuasive impact of the speech.

4. Excessive Filler Words

The habitual use of filler words not only disrupts the flow of communication but also signals a lack of preparation and confidence. It

can lead the audience to question the speaker's command of the subject matter, diminishing their credibility.

5.   Failure to Connect with the Audience

Beyond presenting irrelevant content, failure to connect with the audience involves a lack of relatability and empathy. This disconnect can result in the audience feeling unacknowledged or disengaged, impacting the overall effectiveness of the communication.

6.   Ignoring Vocal Variety

A monotonous tone not only makes the speaker's delivery less engaging but also diminishes the emotional impact of the message. Lack of vocal variety can make it challenging for the audience to connect with the speaker on a deeper level and fully grasp the intended nuances.

7.   Overloading with Information

Presenting an excess of information not only overwhelms the audience but also risks diluting the significance of key points. It reflects a failure to prioritise information effectively and can result in a scattered, confusing narrative.

8.   Reading Directly from Slides or Notes

Over-reliance on written material not only creates a disconnect but also limits the speaker's ability to gauge and respond to the audience's reactions. It can make the presentation feel rehearsed and impersonal, diminishing the speaker's ability to establish a genuine connection.

9.   Ignoring Time Limits

Disregarding time constraints not only disrupts the flow but can also create a negative perception of the speaker's professionalism. Going beyond the allotted time may convey a lack of respect for the audience's schedule, impacting their overall experience.

10. Lack of Adaptability

Inability to adapt not only hinders the speaker's response to unexpected challenges but also reflects a rigid and potentially unprepared

approach. It undermines the speaker's ability to connect with the audience in real-time and adjust the presentation for optimal impact.

Steps for Improving Ability as a Speaker

"All the great speakers were bad speakers at first." - Ralph Waldo Emerson.

THE words above are attributed to the American poet, writer, and lecturer, Ralph Waldo Emerson. It stands to reason that perhaps, some speakers start out better than others, but the bottom line is, we can all improve our public speaking skills.

EFFECTIVE INTRODUCTION

Introductions are important because they provide a first impression, establish credibility with your audience, and prepare the audience for the content of the speech.

What will you accomplish by means of effective introductions? What features should your introductions have?

To pique interest during your speech, use compelling anecdotes, ask thought-provoking questions, incorporate relevant statistics, use quotes or statements, talk about a familiar news item, or employ engaging visuals. Maintaining a dynamic delivery and connecting emotionally with your audience also helps to keep them intrigued.

ANECDOTES

Anecdotes are short, personal stories or accounts that provide insight, humor, or an illustrative example of a point. They are often used to make information more relatable or engaging. Here are some examples of anecdotes that you can use:

> *'Growing up, my grandmother used to tell me captivating bedtime stories that sparked my love for storytelling and inspired me to pursue a career in literature'.*

'Years ago, during a backpacking adventure in Obudu Cattle Ranch, I found myself face-to-face with a rare snow leopard, an encounter that taught me the importance of embracing the unknown'.

'In my early career as a software developer, I once inadvertently deleted a critical piece of code just hours before a major project deadline. The experience taught me valuable lessons about resilience and meticulousness'.

'During my travels in a remote village, I encountered a wise elder who shared a timeless story about unity, leaving a lasting impact on my perspective on teamwork and collaboration'.

'In a challenging moment of my life, a stranger's random act of kindness left a lasting impression on me, illustrating the profound impact simple gestures can have on someone's day'.

QUESTIONS

The following are sample questions to ask when introducing your speech:

1. *'Are you a couple/parent/child?'*

2. *'Did you know?'*

3. *'Have you ever wondered what would happen if we all took a moment each day to appreciate the simple joys that surround us?'*

4. *'Do the small choices we make every day affect the world around us?'*

5. *'How can we make sure that as technology advances, we're doing it in a fair and ethical way?'*

6. *'Balancing technology and personal connections is tricky. How do we find the right mix?'*

7. *'When things get tough, do we see problems as roadblocks or chances to learn and get stronger?'*

STATISTICS

1. 'Studies show that businesses with diverse teams are 35% more likely to outperform their less diverse counterparts in terms of financial performance'.

2. 'On average, people spend more than two hours per day on social media, highlighting the pervasive role it plays in our daily lives'.

3. 'According to recent surveys, over 80% of consumers consider sustainability when making purchasing decisions, emphasising the growing importance of eco-friendly practices in business'.

4. 'Research indicates that regular exercise not only improves physical health but also boosts cognitive function, reducing the risk of age-related mental decline'.

5. 'In the last decade, global internet usage has more than doubled, underlining the increasing interconnectedness of our world and the opportunities it presents for communication and collaboration'.

QUOTES

Using quotes in your speech introduction can be effective because of the following:

1. **Capturing Attention:** Quotes often have a compelling and concise nature, instantly grabbing the audience's attention and setting a tone for the speech.

2. **Credibility:** Leveraging quotes from respected figures lends credibility to your message, as it associates your ideas with well-known and influential individuals.

3. **Emotional Appeal:** Quotes can evoke emotions and resonate with the audience, creating a connection that enhances engagement and understanding.

4. **Condensed Wisdom:** Quotes distil wisdom or insights into a few words, providing a succinct way to convey a powerful message or key concept.

5. **Memorability**: Memorable quotes can stick in the audience's minds, reinforcing your main points and making your speech more memorable overall.

"The only thing we have to fear is fear itself." - Franklin D. Roosevelt

"When you open your mouth, you tell the world who you are." - Les Brown

"In three words I can sum up everything I've learned about life: it goes on." - Robert Frost

"Be the change that you wish to see in the world." - Mahatma Gandhi

"The only limit to our realisation of tomorrow will be our doubts of today." - Franklin D. Roosevelt

"Success is not final; failure is not fatal: It is the courage to continue that counts." - Winston Churchill

---

NEWS ITEM

1. "Recently, groundbreaking research has unveiled a potential breakthrough in renewable energy, promising a significant step towards a sustainable future."

2. "In current headlines, a global initiative is gaining traction to address the challenges of climate change, signalling a collective effort to combat environmental issues."

3. "News reports highlight advancements in artificial intelligence, showcasing the transformative impact on various industries and prompting discussions about ethical considerations."

4. "A recent study on work trends reveals a shift towards remote and flexible work arrangements, emphasising the evolving nature of our professional landscape."

5. "In the tech world, a prominent company's innovative product launch is making waves, reshaping consumer expectations and redefining industry standards."

ENGAGING VISUALS

1. **Infographics:** Create visually appealing infographics to present complex data or statistics in a clear and concise manner. This can help enhance audience understanding.

2. **Charts and Graphs:** To make data more visually engaging, use colourful and well-designed charts and graphs to illustrate trends, comparisons, or patterns.

3. **High-Quality Images:** Incorporate striking images that resonate with your message, evoke emotions, or provide a visual representation of key concepts.

4. **Videos or Animations:** Integrate short videos or animations to add a dynamic element to your presentation, conveying information in a captivating and memorable way.

5. **Mind Maps or Diagrams:** Visualise relationships between ideas using mind maps or diagrams, helping your audience grasp the interconnectedness of concepts in a visually stimulating format.

Your introductions should be able to capture the attention of your audience and prepare them to give favourable consideration to what comes next. One fine way to do this is by getting them involved.

Think about what interests your audience and adapt your introductions accordingly. Let them realise that the information given is important to them, and that it means their life.

State your subject. Your introduction should not only guide the audience into the discussion's core but also distinctly outline the specific aspect of the material you intend to address. It involves narrowing down your subject to a specific theme and, where possible, clearly identifying that theme in your introduction. While an engaging narrative is valuable, it

shouldn't compromise the clarity of your chosen theme. The key is to ensure a seamless connection between the theme introduced in your speech's opening and the subsequent content in order to maintain coherence throughout your presentation.

Well timed. The length of an introduction varies based on factors such as speech duration, purpose, audience, and more. A successful introduction should follow a clear, organised, and engaging sequence of thoughts towards the topic, ensuring completeness without leaving gaps. It's essential to avoid starting too far from the subject, as this may require extensive explanation, prompting the need for a revised introduction and a more suitable starting point.

Consider the context of the event when determining the introduction's length, adjusting it to suit the occasion, whether formal or casual. Additionally, gauge the familiarity of the audience with the topic and tailor your introduction accordingly. A well-crafted introduction not only maintains a logical flow but also captures the audience's attention by incorporating intriguing elements. Remember, striking a balance between depth and conciseness is key, ensuring that your opening sets the stage for the rest of your presentation seamlessly.

PROPER PRONUNCIATION

Effective communication hinges on mastering the art of accurate pronunciation. It plays a pivotal role in enhancing the credibility of public speakers, as eloquent pronunciation imparts a sense of dignity to their discourse.

When speakers neglect the nuances of pronunciation, it becomes a deterrent to their presentation, diverting the audience's attention. However, with dedicated effort, pronunciation challenges can be rectified, allowing listeners to fully engage with the message instead of being distracted by linguistic errors.

Encountering a mispronounced word in a speech acts as a mental roadblock, momentarily derailing focus and prompting reflections on the error rather than the speaker's argument. Undoubtedly, poor pronunciation has the potential to shift attention from the message to the delivery itself, undermining the speaker's intended impact. In my roles as

a speaker, trainer, and coach, I emphasise the importance of precise pronunciation. It is crucial for effective communication.

Improving pronunciation involves familiarising oneself with the sounds of English and utilising resources like dictionaries. For instance, words such as 'phenomenon,' 'entrepreneur,' and 'February' are common stumbling blocks, but mastering their pronunciation contributes significantly to overall communication prowess.

In my pronunciation course—***Pronunciation Prodigy***—I demonstrate these.

CAPTIVATING STORYTELLING

A good story has a powerful effect on the brain and can help retain vital information quickly and longer, both in casual and formal settings. Storytelling does much more than entertain us; it teaches us how to think, feel, and act. In that connection, it is crucial to make good use of this method of teaching.

Brains like stories; in response, they release dopamine (feel good), cortisol (healthy stress to help us focus on the story), and oxytocin (human bonding).

The truth is, when members of the audience aren't listening to a story, their thoughts are scattered. When the story begins, their brain waves synchronise up, uniting your audience.

How can you craft a good story? Follow this pattern. Each has examples.

Think back to when the event actually took place. Create the context within which this event took place. Consider which of the following is relevant to setting the scene for your story:

1. Introduction:

    Time and Place: On a warm summer afternoon in July.

    Atmosphere: The sun bathed the coastal town in a golden glow, creating a relaxed and cheerful ambiance.

2. Character Introduction:

Event: The annual town fair was just around the corner, bringing excitement and anticipation.

Relationships: Sarah, a young entrepreneur, eagerly prepared her handmade crafts to showcase at the fair. Her best friend, Emily, was there to support her.

3. Buildup:

Atmosphere: As the fair approached, the atmosphere buzzed with energy, and the town became a hub of creativity.

Data/Statistics: Local artisans had reported a 20% increase in fair attendance over the previous year.

4. Conflict or Turning Point:

Event: On the day of the fair, unexpected rain clouds loomed, threatening to dampen the outdoor event.

Relationships: Sarah and Emily faced the challenge of protecting their delicate crafts from the rain, testing their friendship and resourcefulness.

5. Resolution:

Atmosphere: Despite the rain, the community rallied, creating an impromptu indoor space for the fair, transforming the atmosphere from tense to resilient.

Event: The fair continued indoors, with attendees appreciating the adaptability of the organisers and the unique charm of the makeshift venue.

Relationships: Sarah and Emily emerged from the experience with a stronger bond, having successfully navigated the unexpected challenge together.

6. Conclusion:

Time and Place: As the rain subsided in the evening, the townsfolk gathered for a spontaneous bonfire on the beach.

Atmosphere: The cool breeze carried the scent of damp earth, creating a sense of camaraderie among the community.

Data/Statistics: Post-fair surveys revealed a high satisfaction rate, solidifying the town's reputation for resilience and creativity.

Storytelling in public speaking is a powerful tool that transcends mere information delivery, creating a captivating and memorable experience for the audience. By weaving narratives into your speech, you establish a deeper connection with listeners and enhance their engagement.

A well-crafted story serves as a vehicle to convey complex ideas in a relatable manner. It humanises your message, making it easier for the audience to connect emotionally. Whether it's a personal anecdote, a relevant case study, or a metaphorical tale, stories add a compelling dimension to your presentation.

Moreover, storytelling aids in retention. People are more likely to remember key points when they are embedded within a narrative. This can be particularly effective in driving home your message and ensuring that your audience leaves with a lasting impression.

An artful storyteller understands the importance of pacing, tone, and gestures. These elements work together to create a dynamic and engaging delivery, holding the audience's attention throughout the narrative. When executed skillfully, storytelling transforms your speech from a monologue to a shared experience, fostering a sense of connection and resonance with your listeners.

In essence, incorporating storytelling into public speaking elevates your communication from a simple exchange of information to a compelling and memorable performance that leaves a lasting impact.

Crafting a compelling story involves several key elements to capture your audience's attention and make your narrative impactful. Here are some tips to help you create a good story:

What should you think about when crafting a story?

1. Know Your Audience

    Tailor your story to resonate with your specific audience. Consider their interests, values, and experiences to make the narrative more relatable.

2. Establish a Clear Purpose

    Define the purpose of your story. Whether it's to entertain, inspire, or educate, clarity on your objective will guide the content and tone of your narrative.

3. Create a Strong Opening

    Begin with a captivating hook to grab your audience's attention from the start. This could be a question, a surprising fact, or a vivid description that sets the scene.

4. Develop Engaging Characters

    Introduce characters with whom your audience can connect emotionally. Develop their personalities, challenges, and aspirations to add depth to your story.

5. Build a Compelling Plot

    Construct a well-paced plot that includes a beginning, middle, and end. Introduce conflict or tension to keep your audience interested, leading to a satisfying resolution.

6. Use Descriptive Language

    Paint a vivid picture with descriptive language. Engage the senses to help your audience visualise and feel the events of the story.

7. Incorporate Dialogue

    Dialogue adds authenticity and brings characters to life. Use direct quotes when possible and ensure conversations contribute to the overall narrative flow.

8. **Include a Climax and Resolution**

   Build towards a climactic moment that holds your audience's attention. Follow it with a resolution that provides closure and reinforces the main message or lesson.

9. **Connect to a Larger Message**

   Relate your story to the broader theme or message you want to convey. This helps your audience see the relevance and significance of the narrative.

10. **Practice and Refine**

    Practise delivering your story to ensure smooth and confident delivery. Pay attention to pacing, tone, and gestures to enhance the overall impact.

PAUSING

Pausing is one of the most overlooked delivery techniques, but there are many benefits of using pauses effectively. It is crucial that pauses are placed properly. Without such pauses, there will be no lasting impression. Accordingly, it is vital to note that pausing helps to impart clarity of speech, and makes your points stand out.

What are the benefits of pausing?

Maintaining a seamless flow in your speech allows your audience to stay connected, as speaking without pauses forces them to expend effort keeping up. Conversely, well-placed pauses provide valuable moments for reflection and personal connection, forming the foundation of audience engagement.

Ensure your listeners comprehend your message by incorporating complete stops at appropriate intervals. Brief pauses or subtle fades in your delivery allow your audience to process the information and establish personal connections with their own experiences.

According to researcher Brigitte Zellner, pauses serve as speech beacons, structuring the entire utterance for both the speaker and the listener.

These intentional pauses contribute significantly to improved speech comprehension by subdividing the content into smaller, digestible segments.

Strategically applied pauses are beneficial for your well-being, allowing moments for deep breaths, swallowing, or taking a sip of water. Beyond supporting cognitive function, maintaining a well-lubricated mouth and throat throughout your speech enhances vocal quality.

Consider incorporating pauses in specific situations, such as during transitions. Pausing during a shift from one point to another not only prevents disorientation but also provides your audience with a moment to reflect on the transition, fostering clarity and understanding.

Additionally, use pauses to punctuate your spoken words, offering cues to your audience about the conclusion of a phrase, sentence, or paragraph. In the absence of visual cues like punctuation marks, your intentional pauses serve as vital indicators, helping your audience follow the flow and structure of your speech.

GESTURES

The significance of body movement in public speaking is frequently overlooked. Gestures and facial expressions not only visually enhance your speech but also contribute emotional emphasis, infusing vitality into your voice.

Gestures play a crucial role in reinforcing the meaning of your words, supplementing and vitalizing your ideas. Almost everyone naturally incorporates some form of gesturing while speaking.

Onstage, the absence of gestures signals unease to your audience. Conversely, when you gesture authentically, your audience focuses on your message rather than on you. Natural gestures animate your presentation, stirring up emotions and adding vibrancy to your delivery. Gestures, when appropriately used, help you achieve the following:

Support your message. Enhance your message by aligning full-body movement with your words, adding emphasis and depth to your presentation.

Increase authenticity. Boost authenticity by allowing natural movement when you're genuinely passionate about your message. Remaining overly static may raise doubts about your sincerity and connection with the content.

Enable balanced audience connection. As you move from the centre of the speaking area to the left or to the right, full-body movement brings you closer to different audience members. By reducing the separation distance, you will increase your ability to connect with your audience in a balanced way.

Own the stage. Seize control of the stage, utilising the entire speaking area to amplify your presentation. Rather than confining yourself to a single spot, embracing the stage symbolically reinforces your ownership of the space.

Attract audience attention. Body movement is the largest physical gesture that you can make (i.e. it's "bigger" than gestures with your hands, face, or eyes). For this reason, any full-body movement tends to immediately attract attention from your audience.

Dissipate nervous energy. If you are stationary for too long, then your body will gravitate toward distracting oscillating movements (see below for examples) as a means of expending nervous energy. Purposeful body movement will dissipate this energy in a non-distracting way.

Avoid muscle stagnation. If you lock your knees and plant your feet for long periods of time, your muscles can tighten up. Occasional body movements avoid this and keep your blood pumping. By caring for your physical needs, you are able to deliver your best speech possible!

EFFECTIVE CONCLUSION

An effective conclusion not only reinforces key points and delivers a strong final message but also motivates your audience to reflect, remember, and take meaningful action.

In addition to drawing sharp focus on key points and driving home the theme, an effective conclusion in public speaking should:

Summarise Key Points: Recapitulate the main ideas or arguments presented throughout your speech. This reinforces the core message and aids in memory retention for the audience.

Reiterate the Purpose: Remind the audience of the speech's purpose or objective. Clearly articulate what you aimed to achieve, emphasising the significance of the information shared.

Create a Memorable Ending: Craft a memorable closing statement or anecdote that leaves a lasting impression. A powerful ending enhances the overall impact of your message and ensures that your speech is remembered vividly.

Call to Action: Encourage your audience to take specific actions based on the information presented. Whether it's adopting a new perspective, implementing a solution, or further exploring a topic, a well-articulated call to action motivates your audience to engage with your message beyond the speech.

Provide Closure: Signal the end of your speech clearly. Avoid introducing new information or raising additional questions in the conclusion. Provide a sense of closure that leaves your audience with a feeling of satisfaction and completeness.

Connect with the Introduction: Create a sense of unity by tying your conclusion back to the introduction. This circular structure reinforces your overall message and leaves a cohesive impression on your audience.

Use Emotional Appeal: Consider incorporating emotional elements in your conclusion. Whether it's a personal story, a quote, or a powerful statement, appealing to emotions adds resonance to your message.

Invite Questions or Discussion: If appropriate for the context, invite questions or open the floor for discussion. This engagement fosters a connection with your audience and allows for further exploration of the topic.

Bonus Steps

Mastering the art of public speaking requires a multifaceted approach. First, you must remember that your speech is not always about you. Stop

putting yourself in the picture and start putting the interest of your listeners at heart. It is important to invest ample time in understanding your audience. You also have to realise that the more you speak, the better you become.

VISUALISE SUCCESS

What is involved in visualising success? Visualising success involves creating a vivid mental image of yourself successfully accomplishing a specific goal or task. When you visualise, your mind does not know the difference between what is happening in your reality in the now and what you are creating in your imagination. It's a technique that harnesses the power of imagination to mentally rehearse a positive outcome.

The key to effective visualisation is to make it as detailed and realistic as possible. To help you understand the concept, think of the following:

Imagine you have an upcoming public speaking engagement. To visualise success, follow these steps:

1. **Find a Quiet Space:** Sit or lie down in a quiet, comfortable space where you won't be disturbed.

2. **Close Your Eyes:** Close your eyes to eliminate external distractions and focus inward.

3. **Deep Breaths:** Take a few deep, calming breaths to relax your body and mind.

4. **Set the Scene:** Imagine yourself standing confidently on the stage, with the audience in front of you. Picture the room, the podium, and the faces of the people listening.

5. **Engage Your Senses:** Make the visualisation as vivid as possible. Imagine the lights on your face, the feel of the podium under your hands, the sound of your voice echoing through the room.

6. **Feel the Emotions:** Experience the positive emotions associated with success. Feel the confidence, the pride, and the sense of accomplishment.

7. **Visualise Success:** Picture yourself delivering your speech with poise and clarity. Picture the audience engaged and responsive, nodding in agreement or applauding. You can imagine a standing ovation, picture the smiles on the faces of the members of the audience, and hear how others are sharing with you what an amazing job you did.

8. **Anticipate Challenges:** If there are potential challenges or obstacles, visualise yourself handling them with grace and confidence. See yourself adapting and continuing with your speech.

9. **Celebrate the Success:** Imagine the sense of achievement and satisfaction you'll feel after delivering a successful presentation.

Here's an illustrative scenario:

You see yourself on stage, under the spotlight. Your posture is strong, and you maintain eye contact with the audience. Your voice is clear and steady, conveying your message with conviction. As you speak, you notice the audience nodding in agreement, showing signs of engagement and appreciation. You navigate through your points seamlessly, even addressing a minor interruption with calmness and professionalism.

After finishing your speech, you feel a surge of pride and accomplishment. The audience applauds, and you leave the stage with a sense of fulfilment, knowing you delivered a successful presentation.

The more you visualise that outcome the more the brain will try to reproduce it because it will see that as a reality.

Many people, from speakers or performers, to professional athletes, use visualisation. As you get closer to the day of the event, visualise it every night before you go to bed and when you get up in the morning. This will help create the routine and solidify in your mind the success you will have.

KNOW YOUR WHY AND CONSTANTLY REMIND YOURSELF OF IT

Knowing your "why" refers to understanding the deeper purpose, values, and motivations that drive your actions and decisions. It's about gaining clarity on what truly matters to you, what you are passionate about, and what gives your life meaning. This concept is often associated with personal development, leadership, and goal-setting, as it can provide a guiding framework for making choices that align with your values and long-term objectives.

Here are some key aspects of knowing your "why" and reminding yourself of it:

1. **Self-Reflection:**

    Take time to reflect on your values, beliefs, and priorities. Ask yourself fundamental questions about what you want to achieve in life and what kind of person you want to become.

2. **Identifying Values:**

    Determine the values that are most important to you. These could be principles such as honesty, integrity, creativity, or service to others. Your "why" often stems from these core values.

3. **Setting Goals:**

    Align your goals with your "why." When your objectives are connected to a deeper purpose, you are more likely to stay motivated and focused on your path.

4. **Finding Passion:**

    Explore your passions and interests. Knowing your "why" involves understanding what activities or causes ignite a sense of purpose and fulfilment in you.

5. **Creating a Personal Mission Statement:**

    Develop a personal mission statement that succinctly captures your values, goals, and purpose. This statement can serve as a constant reminder of your "why."

6. **Reminding Yourself:**

    Regularly revisit and remind yourself of your "why." This can involve daily or weekly reflections, creating visual reminders, or incorporating your "why" into your routine.

7. **Making Decisions:**

    Use your "why" as a decision-making guide. When faced with choices, consider whether they align with your deeper purpose and values.

8. **Adapting to Change:**

    As circumstances and priorities evolve, be open to reassessing your "why" and adjusting it accordingly. Flexibility is essential for personal growth.

9. **Sharing Your Why:**

    Communicate your "why" with others, such as friends, family, or colleagues. Sharing your purpose can create accountability and support from those around you.

10. **Overcoming Challenges:**

    During difficult times, your "why" can serve as a source of resilience. Remind yourself of the bigger picture and how challenges align with your overall journey.

Knowing your "why" is an ongoing process that requires self-awareness, reflection, and a commitment to living in alignment with your values. It's a powerful tool for creating a meaningful and purpose-driven life.

Ask yourself: 'Why do I want to speak to people?', 'In what way do I want to help others?' If you have a big enough reason why, it will help reduce anxiety.

CREATE A RITUAL

Research underscores the impact of rituals on our psychological state and how they can serve as practical tools to enhance performance and well-being across different aspects of life.

Creating a routine has made a big difference for me. When I struggled with sleeping, for example, I started a simple bedtime ritual—dimming lights, listening to refreshing songs, and reading a calming book. Surprisingly, my body got the message that it was time to sleep, making bedtime more peaceful.

This showed me how routines offer comfort and signal our minds for a specific state. I took this idea to my work life, especially before presentations. I picked a motivating song as my pre-presentation anthem (amongst other artistes, I enjoy listening to NF). Listening to his songs before practising not only pumps me up but also becomes a mental cue for a confident and focused mindset.

Simple routines, like the calming bedtime ritual and the empowering pre-presentation tradition, proves how these habits can be powerful tools, affecting both our mindset and performance. Exploring and refining these routines has shown me the real impact intentional habits can have on our well-being and success.

Because we are all creatures of habits, we can use habits or rituals to get us in the right state of mind. Establishing a ritual can significantly impact our mental state and can leverage our innate inclination toward habits. Consider the exercise ritual: when you consistently incorporate physical activity into your routine, your body adapts, and your mind recognizes the upcoming exertion. Studies indicate that rituals, like a pre-workout routine, have the potential to enhance performance by priming both the body and mind for the upcoming activity.

These rituals establish a sense of anticipation and preparation, signalling to your brain that it's time to transition into a specific mode. Just as athletes have pre-game rituals to optimise their mental and physical state, individuals in various domains can benefit from purposeful routines.

Whether it's a few moments of focused breathing before a crucial meeting or a specific warm-up routine before a creative session, these rituals contribute to a smoother transition between tasks and an improved overall experience.

Moreover, the concept of rituals extends beyond immediate performance benefits. Studies reveal that engaging in rituals consistently over time can contribute to the development of a positive mindset and increased resilience. For instance, a daily gratitude ritual, where you reflect on things you're thankful for, has been linked to improved mental well-being and stress reduction.

Rituals, it seems, not only shape our immediate experiences but also play a role in our long-term psychological resilience. The repetition and predictability inherent in rituals provide a sense of stability and control, factors that are crucial in navigating the uncertainties of daily life. As we embrace and incorporate rituals into our routines, we create a foundation for psychological well-being that extends far beyond the specific activities involved.

In essence, the evidence suggests that rituals serve as both immediate performance enhancers and long-term contributors to our mental and emotional resilience, offering a dual benefit in our quest for a balanced and fulfilling life.

GET INTO CHARACTER

Another tool that some presenters use is to create a character that they 'play' during their presentation, and so when they are going to do a presentation, they 'get into character'. This character may have a nickname and it has the characteristics you want to have, that would make you feel confident. What would be this character's actions, thoughts, and mannerisms?

Once you determine your character, embody them whenever you practise; that way it is easier to become that character when you have to perform. Getting into character for a presentation is a powerful technique that can significantly enhance your confidence, creativity, and connection, and impact with your audience. Here are several reasons why it is important to create and embody a character for your presentation:

1. ***Boosts Confidence:*** Adopting a character allows you to step outside of your comfort zone and assume a role that embodies confidence and competence. This psychological shift can boost your self-esteem and make you feel more secure and capable during the presentation.

2. ***Enhances Authenticity:*** Ironically, creating a character can make your presentation more authentic. By selecting qualities and traits that resonate with you, you are infusing a genuine part of yourself into the character. This authenticity can make your presentation more relatable and engaging for the audience.

3. ***Improves Memorization:*** When you associate information with a character, it becomes easier to remember. The act of embodying the character during practice helps reinforce key points, making it more likely that you will recall them effortlessly during the actual presentation.

4. ***Increases Creativity:*** Developing a character encourages creativity in your presentation approach. You have the freedom to experiment with different communication styles, tones, and gestures that may not come naturally to you. This creativity can make your presentation more dynamic and memorable.

5. ***Establishes a Persona:*** Your character can serve as a consistent persona that your audience can connect with. This establishes a recognizable identity for your presentations, making it easier for your audience to remember and engage with your content.

6. ***Manages Nervous Energy:*** Nervous energy is a common challenge when presenting. Channelling this energy into your character allows you to use it constructively. Your character becomes a vessel for the nervous energy, transforming it into enthusiasm and dynamism that can captivate your audience.

7. ***Provides a Mental Cue:*** Having a specific character as a reference provides a mental cue for your brain to switch into presentation mode. It signals a shift in mindset from everyday activities to the focused and confident demeanour required for a successful presentation.

8. ***Encourages Consistency:*** Consistency is key in effective communication. By adopting a character, you establish a consistent framework for your presentations. This helps in maintaining a uniform style and tone across different speaking engagements.

9. ***Fosters Connection with the Audience:*** A well-defined character can create a personal connection with your audience. If your character embodies relatable qualities, the audience is more likely to connect with you on a human level, enhancing the overall impact of your presentation.

By embracing this technique, you transform the act of presenting into an engaging and authentic performance.

ACCEPTANCE

In the journey of personal growth and self-discovery, a profound principle has become a guiding light in my life—"You only get more of what you resist." This wisdom encourages us to embrace challenges, emotions, and situations rather than resist them. Through acceptance, we find the path to transformation and resilience.

How To Prepare Your Speech

Preparing your speech is a crucial part of delivering an effective presentation. Here are some additional details on how to prepare your speech:

1. Choose a topic: The first step in preparing your speech is to choose a topic that is relevant and engaging to your audience. Consider the purpose of your speech and what you want to communicate to your audience.

2. Research: Once you have a topic, conduct research to gather information and data that will support your message. Look for credible sources such as academic journals, books, and reputable websites.

3. Organise your thoughts: After you have gathered your research, organise your thoughts and ideas into a clear and logical structure.

This can include creating an outline, mapping out key points, and identifying supporting evidence.

4. **Develop a clear message:** It's important to have a clear and consistent message throughout your speech. Develop a central idea or thesis statement that will guide your speech and help you stay on topic.

5. **Use visual aids:** Visual aids such as slides, props, or handouts can help enhance your presentation and engage your audience. Make sure your visual aids are clear, concise, and relevant to your message.

6. **Practise:** Practise your speech multiple times to become comfortable with the content and delivery. Practice in front of a mirror or record yourself to identify areas that may need improvement.

7. **Get feedback:** Ask friends or colleagues to watch your practice sessions and provide feedback. Use their feedback to make improvements to your delivery and content.

CHAPTER 5

BUSINESS WRITING

When it comes to business writing, many people think it is just about following formal templates, but it is much more than that. The foundation of excellent business writing lies in effective communication. You want to be clear, concise, and confident in what you are conveying, whether it is a simple email to a colleague or a detailed proposal to a client.

This chapter covers the basics—the very building blocks of professional writing.

Understanding the Purpose of Business Writing

Why Do We Write in Business? Think about it: you are sending an email to your manager requesting time off. You would not write it the same way you would text your friend. Business writing serves a purpose—it helps get things done by communicating clearly to the right people.

For example:

- **Requesting information**: Asking a client for feedback on a product.

- **Giving instructions**: Emailing your team about a new policy.

- **Providing information**: Sending a report to update stakeholders on a project.

- **Persuading**: Writing a proposal to convince a potential partner.

Different tasks require different writing styles, but the goal is the same—communicating clearly to get results.

Example: You need to write an email to your boss, Mr. Kamau, requesting time off:

- **Casual Email**: "Hey, I won't be in next week. Can I take off?"

- **Business Email**: "Dear Mr. Kamau, I would like to request leave from the 10th to the 13th of this month. Please let me know if this is convenient."

Both emails ask for the same thing, but the second is formal, respectful, and professional, fitting for a business environment.

Aligning Your Writing with Your Audience

The key to good business writing is knowing your audience. Writing to your colleague, Juma, is different from writing to your boss, Ms. Njeri. Your tone, style, and content need to adjust depending on who is reading.

Understanding the Audience's Needs: Imagine you are writing an update email. If you are writing to your customers, the focus will be on how changes affect them. But if you are writing to your internal team, you will emphasise the technical aspects and next steps.

Practical Tip: Before you start writing, always ask yourself:

- *Who am I writing to?*

- *What do they need to know?*

- *What's the main message I want them to understand?*

Example: You have to inform your team and clients about a delay in the launch of a service. Here's how your approach changes:

- *To Clients:*
  "Dear Mr. Otieno, we regret to inform you that the launch of our new service will be delayed by one week due to unforeseen circumstances. We sincerely apologise for any inconvenience this may cause and assure you that we are working to resolve the issue promptly."

- *To Team Members:*
  "Hi Team, the launch of the new service has been pushed back by one week because of some technical challenges. Please focus on

troubleshooting and testing to make sure this doesn't happen again. Let's meet tomorrow to regroup and plan the way forward."

See the difference? To the client, you are polite and reassuring. To your team, you are more direct, focusing on action.

The 7 Cs of Effective Business Writing

These seven principles are your guide to writing effectively in a business context. Think of them as the golden rules to follow for clear, professional communication.

Let's break them down with some examples:

1. **Clarity**: Your writing should be easy to understand. Avoid complex language when simple words will work.
   Example:
   Instead of:
   "We would appreciate your prompt remittance of the outstanding balance at your earliest convenience."
   Write:
   "Please pay the outstanding balance as soon as possible."

2. **Conciseness**: Get to the point quickly. Remove unnecessary words and phrases.
   Example:
   Instead of:
   "Due to the fact that the project has been delayed, we are unable to proceed."
   Write:
   "Since the project is delayed, we cannot proceed."

3. **Coherence**: Make sure your writing flows logically from one point to the next. Each sentence should connect clearly to the previous one.
   Example:
   When explaining a process:
   "First, log into the system. Next, click on 'Reports'. Then, select the report format."

4. **Consistency**: Maintain a consistent tone and style throughout your writing. Do not switch from formal to informal halfway through.

5. **Correctness**: Proofread to ensure that your writing is free from grammatical errors. Accuracy is crucial in business communication.

6. **Courtesy**: Always be polite, even when discussing difficult topics. Being courteous will help you maintain professional relationships.
Example:
Instead of:
"You didn't submit the report on time."
Write:
"I noticed the report was not submitted by the deadline. Could you please provide an update?"

7. **Completeness**: Ensure that all necessary information is included so the recipient does not need to ask for clarification.
Example:
If you are sending an invoice:
"Please find attached the invoice for the services provided. Kindly ensure payment is made by 25th September."

Practical Exercises

Here are some activities to help solidify the concepts:

1. **Rewrite for Clarity**:
Original: *"The team members have indicated a preference for a more streamlined approach to the project in light of recent developments."*
Try: *"The team prefers a simpler approach to the project after recent changes."*

2. **Identify Your Audience**:
Write an email asking for feedback on a new service. Then, imagine you are sending it to two different audiences: one to a colleague, Wanjiku, and another to a client, Mr. Muthoni. Notice how the tone changes.

- ***To Colleague:***
  "Hi Wanjiku, could you share your thoughts on the new service launch? Is there anything we should improve?"

- ***To Client:***
  "Dear Mr. Muthoni, we would appreciate your feedback on our newly launched service. Your insights will help us make it better."

Effective Writing: What to Do vs. What to Avoid

1. Clarity vs. Ambiguity

Do: Use clear and precise language that leaves no room for misunderstanding. When writing effectively, your message should be straightforward, so the reader knows exactly what you mean. For example, *"Please submit your report by 5 PM on Friday."*

Don't: Use vague or ambiguous terms that could confuse the reader. Ambiguity often arises when instructions or statements are open to multiple interpretations, leading to uncertainty about what's required. For example, *"Submit your report as soon as possible."* This phrase is ambiguous because it doesn't specify a deadline, leaving the reader unsure of the urgency.

2. Conciseness vs. Wordiness

Do: Be concise and get straight to the point. Effective writing communicates ideas clearly without unnecessary words, making it easier for the reader to grasp the message. For example, *"The meeting starts at 9 AM."*

Don't: Overload your sentences with unnecessary words or filler phrases. Wordiness can dilute your message and make it harder for the reader to identify the key points. For example, *"The meeting is scheduled to start at 9 AM in the morning, and we would appreciate it if everyone could be there on time."* This is wordy because phrases like *"in the morning"* and *"we would appreciate it if"* add no significant value.

3. Active Voice vs. Passive Voice

Do: Use active voice to make your writing more dynamic and direct. Active sentences often feel more engaging and powerful, as they clearly identify the action and the doer. For example, *"The manager approved the budget."*

Don't: Overuse passive voice, which can make your writing seem weak or indirect. Passive voice often hides the subject performing the action, leading to a less clear and less compelling sentence. For example, *"The budget was approved by the manager."* This is less effective because it shifts the focus away from the subject.

4. Specificity vs. Generalisation

Do: Use specific details to support your points and make your writing more convincing. Specificity adds credibility and helps the reader understand exactly what you mean. For example, *"Our sales increased by 15% in the last quarter."*

Don't: Make general statements without backing them up with facts or specifics. Generalisation can make your writing vague and less persuasive, as the reader is left without concrete information. For example, *"Our sales did very well last quarter."* This is generalised because it doesn't provide a clear measure of success.

5. Proper Structure vs. Poor Organisation

Do: Organise your writing with a clear structure, using paragraphs, headings, and transitions. A well-structured piece of writing guides the reader through your ideas logically. For example, starting with an introduction, followed by supporting details, and ending with a conclusion provides a clear flow.

Don't: Write without a logical flow, jumping from one idea to another without connecting them. Poor organisation can confuse the reader and obscure your main points. For example, discussing the conclusion before explaining the supporting details can disrupt the reader's understanding.

6. Strong Word Choice vs. Weak Vocabulary

Do: Choose strong, impactful words that convey your message powerfully. The right word can add emphasis and make your writing more memorable. For example, *"The proposal was rejected due to its high costs."*

Don't: Use weak or overused words that dilute your message. Weak vocabulary can make your writing feel bland and uninspired. For example, *"The proposal was not accepted because it was too expensive."* This is weak because it lacks the punch that stronger word choices could provide.

7. Engagement vs. Monotony

Do: Engage your reader with varied sentence structures and interesting content. Variety keeps the reader's attention and makes your writing more enjoyable to read. For example, *"Our innovative approach led to a 20% increase in productivity."*

Don't: Write in a monotonous tone that could bore your reader. Monotony can make your writing feel tedious and unengaging. For example, *"Our method led to some improvements."* This sentence is monotonous because it lacks detail and energy.

8. Correct Grammar and Punctuation vs. Errors

Do: Use correct grammar and punctuation to ensure your writing is professional and easy to read. Proper grammar helps to avoid confusion and maintains the credibility of your writing. For example, *"Let's discuss the details in tomorrow's meeting."*

Don't: Ignore grammar and punctuation rules, leading to confusion or misinterpretation. Errors in grammar or punctuation can distract the reader and undermine your message. For example, *"Lets discuss the details in tomorrows meeting."* This is incorrect because it lacks the necessary apostrophes.

9. Appropriate Tone vs. Misjudged Tone

Do: Match your tone to your audience and purpose. The right tone ensures that your message is received in the spirit it was intended. For

example, in a business proposal, a formal tone is appropriate: *"We are confident this plan will benefit all stakeholders."*

Don't: Use an inappropriate tone that might offend or alienate your audience. Misjudged tone can lead to misunderstandings or a negative response. For example, using slang or overly casual language in a business context: *"This plan is a total win for everyone."* This might come across as unprofessional.

10. Revising and Editing vs. First Draft Submission

Do: Revise and edit your writing to improve clarity, correctness, and impact. Taking the time to polish your work ensures that it's the best it can be. For example, *"After reviewing the document, I noticed a few areas for improvement."*

Don't: Submit your first draft without reviewing or making necessary corrections. Skipping the revision process can result in errors and weaken your writing. For example, submitting work with typos, unclear sentences, or factual errors shows a lack of attention to detail.

Mastering Email Etiquette and Professional Correspondence

You know how they say you never get a second chance to make a first impression? Well, that holds true in email communication as well. Whether you are writing to a client, your boss, or a colleague, the way you craft your email can either open doors or close them. So, in this section, we are going to demystify email etiquette and turn you into an email-writing pro. Together, we will cover structure, common pitfalls, and how to strike the perfect tone—polite, professional, and relatable.

Crafting a Polished Professional Email

Writing a great email is like setting the stage for a productive conversation. You would not just barge into someone's office and start talking, right? Your email needs to follow a structure that ensures clarity and professionalism. Here is a simple breakdown:

Subject Line: Your email's handshake.

Keep it concise yet informative. Avoid vague titles that leave the recipient guessing.

- **Example**: Instead of *"Quick Question,"* try *"Follow-Up on Q4 Sales Report"*. It is clear, relevant, and gets straight to the point.

Greeting: Set the right tone from the start.

Who you are addressing will dictate the level of formality.

- **Formal**: "Dear Mr. Kamau,"

- **Casual (but still professional)**: "Hi Brenda,"

Opening Line: Warm it up.

Start on a friendly note without being overly familiar.

- **Example**: *"I hope this email finds you well,"* or *"I'm writing to follow up on our conversation."*

Body: Get to the heart of your message.

Here, you need to be clear and concise, sticking to the point without unnecessary details.

- **Example**: *"I'm writing to confirm the project deadline for next Monday. Please let me know if any adjustments are needed."*

Closing Line: Leave them with a positive vibe.

End on a courteous note that leaves the door open for further communication.

- **Example**: *"I look forward to your feedback,"* or *"Thank you for your time and attention."*

Sign-Off: A strong finish is key.

Choose a professional but friendly sign-off.

- **Formal**: "Kind regards," or "Sincerely,"
- **Casual**: "Best," or "Warm regards,"

Dodging Common Email Blunders

We have all received emails that made us cringe—maybe because they were too casual, riddled with errors, or simply confusing. Avoiding these common mistakes will help ensure that your emails always hit the right note.

1. Unclear Subject Lines

    Your subject line should be direct and specific.

    Example: *"Update on September Meeting Agenda"* is far better than just *"Update."*

2. Overly Casual Tone with Formal Contacts

    You might have a friendly rapport with a client, but that does not mean you should sound like you are texting them. Keep the tone professional.

    Example:

    - **Too Casual**: *"Hey, can we push the meeting?"*

    - **Better**: *"Dear Mr. Njoroge, could we reschedule our meeting to a more convenient time?"*

3. Neglecting Proofreading

    A single typographical error can ruin an otherwise polished email. Always take a moment to proofread.

    Example: Instead of writing *"Please fined the document attached,"* ensure it says *"Please find the document attached."*

4. All Caps = Shouting

    Writing in all caps feels aggressive. Keep it calm and professional.

    Example:

- **Aggressive**: *"PLEASE SEE ATTACHED FILE!"*
- **Better**: *"Please see the attached file."*

5. Using "Reply All" Unnecessarily

Avoid cluttering inboxes. Only use "Reply All" when everyone on the email thread genuinely needs to see your response.

Striking the Right Tone in Emails

Tone is everything in email communication. No matter the situation—whether you are sending a thank-you note, delivering bad news, or addressing a complaint—maintaining a polite and professional tone is essential.

1. Always Use "Please" and "Thank You"

    Courtesy is a sign of professionalism. Even simple phrases can elevate the tone of your email.

    Example: *"Could you please share the revised document?"* and *"Thank you for your help."*

2. Apologising Gracefully

    Mistakes happen, and a sincere apology can go a long way.

    Example: *"I apologise for the delayed response. I will get back to you by the end of today."*

3. Maintaining Neutrality in Sensitive Situations

    If you are delivering bad news or addressing a contentious issue, keep your tone neutral and focus on solutions.

    Example:

    - **Too Harsh**: *"Your team missed the deadline completely."*

    - **Better**: *"It seems there was a delay with the submission. Can we work together to resolve this?"*

Tailoring Emails for Different Audiences

The person you are writing to should always influence the tone and style of your email. Here are examples of how you might adapt your message depending on who is reading it.

Scenario 1: Emailing a Colleague (David)
You need to ask your colleague David for a quick update on a project.

> *"Hey David, hope your day is going well. Just checking in to see if you've had a chance to review the project plan. Let me know if you need anything from me."*

Notice the friendly yet professional tone.

Scenario 2: Emailing a Client (Mrs. Wambui)
You need to inform Mrs. Wambui about a shipment delay.

> *"Dear Mrs. Wambui, I hope you are doing well. I wanted to inform you that the shipment of your order has been delayed due to unforeseen circumstances. We deeply apologise for any inconvenience this may cause and are working to expedite the process."*

Formal, clear, and respectful.

Scenario 3: Emailing Your Manager (Mr. Kimani)
You are submitting a report to your boss and want to keep the message concise yet respectful.

> *"Dear Mr. Kimani, I have attached the sales report as requested. Please let me know if there is anything else you would like me to add or adjust."*

Professional and to the point.

Handling Tough Emails with Finesse

Sometimes, you will have to send emails that are less than pleasant—like delivering bad news or addressing complaints. The key is to stay calm, professional, and solution-oriented.

Scenario 1: Delivering Bad News (Mr. Otieno)
You need to inform Mr. Otieno that his project will be delayed.

> *"Dear Mr. Otieno, I regret to inform you that there will be a delay of one week in delivering the project due to technical issues. We are actively working on a solution and will keep you updated. We sincerely apologise for the inconvenience."*

Scenario 2: Responding to a Complaint (Ms. Nduta)
Ms. Nduta has raised a concern about the quality of a service.

> *"Dear Ms. Nduta, thank you for bringing this matter to our attention. We sincerely apologise for the inconvenience caused. We are investigating the issue and will ensure that it is addressed promptly. Your feedback is important to us, and we appreciate your understanding."*

Practical Email Writing Exercises

Now that we have covered the essentials, let us put this knowledge into practice:

1. **Rewriting for Professionalism**
   Original: *"Send the file by tomorrow."*
   Better: *"Could you please send the file by tomorrow?"*

2. **Adapting for Different Recipients**
   Write an email asking for feedback on a project. Then, adjust it for three different audiences:

3. **Colleague**: *"Hi Faith, any thoughts on the updated project draft? Feel free to let me know if you want to add anything."*

4. **Client**: *"Dear Mr. Muriithi, I would appreciate your feedback on the attached project draft. Please let me know if you have any comments or suggestions."*

5. **Boss**: *"Dear Ms. Wairimu, I've attached the latest project draft for your review. Kindly share any feedback at your convenience."*

Email Structure and Format

Written communication is like the unsung hero of professional life. Whether you are sending an email, drafting a report, or writing a memo, the way you communicate in writing speaks volumes about your professionalism. It is not just about getting words onto a page; it is about making sure those words convey your message clearly, concisely, and appropriately to your audience. Let us break it down and explore how you can excel in written communication, adapting your style to different audiences.

Writing Clear, Concise, and Professional Emails, Reports, or Memos

When writing professionally, clarity is your best friend. No one wants to sift through paragraphs of unnecessary information to understand what you are trying to say. Your goal is to make your message as straightforward as possible.

- Clarity: Clear writing means your reader understands your point immediately. Imagine you are sending an email to a colleague about an upcoming meeting. Rather than writing, "The meeting we discussed earlier, which is in relation to the new project, has been scheduled," you could simply say, "The meeting about the new project is scheduled for Friday at 10 a.m." The latter is much easier to digest because it is direct and clear.

- Conciseness: Being concise means cutting out any fluff. Think of conciseness like trimming a tree: you want to remove the excess leaves to expose the strong branches underneath. If you are writing a report, avoid overly complicated sentences that make your message harder to understand. Instead of writing, "It is important to note that due to the nature of the current circumstances, we are facing challenges that may or may not impact the overall outcome," you could say, "The current situation may affect the outcome." It gets straight to the point without any extra padding.

- **Professionalism:** Professional tone matters in emails, reports, or memos. Always start with a proper salutation, use polite language, and close appropriately. Let us say you are writing a memo to your team. Instead of starting with, "Hey guys, just a quick note," you should use a more formal tone, such as, "Dear Team, I would like to update you on..." It sets the right tone and shows respect for your audience.

How To Write Reports, Memos, And Proposals, Like A Professional

Professional writing and reporting are essential for clear communication, decision-making, and transparency in a business. They reflect a company's credibility and professionalism. This section offers guidelines and examples to improve these vital skills in the workplace. In this section, I use the Tech industry as a model.

Memos

MEMORANDUM

To: All Staff
From: Adeola Okoro, HR Manager
Date: 10th August 2024
Subject: Mandatory Staff Training

Please be informed that a mandatory staff training session on Data Privacy and Security will be held on 22nd August 2024, from 9:00 AM to 12:00 PM in the Conference Room. Attendance is compulsory for all employees.

The training aims to enhance our understanding of data protection regulations and best practices for safeguarding sensitive company information.

Kindly treat this as urgent.

Minutes

Minutes of the Sales Team Meeting

Date: 8th August 2024
Time: 10:00 AM
Location: Conference Room

Attendees:

- Adewale Ojo (Sales Manager)
- Bolaji Adebayo (Sales Representative)
- Chioma Nwafor (Sales Representative)
- Diran Olanrewaju (Sales Representative)

Absent:

- Femi Akintola (Sales Representative) – on leave

Discussions:

1. Review of Q3 sales performance
2. Launch of the new product line, SmartTech
3. Sales targets for Q4
4. Customer feedback analysis

Decisions:

- Develop a targeted marketing campaign for the SmartTech product line.
- Set aggressive but achievable sales targets for Q4.
- Implement a customer relationship management (CRM) system to improve customer engagement.

Action Items:

- Adewale to prepare a detailed marketing plan for SmartTech.
- Bolaji to lead the CRM system implementation project.
- All sales representatives to conduct customer satisfaction surveys.

Next Meeting: 22nd August 2024, 10:00 AM

Report

Mobile App User Acquisition Strategy
TechBridge Solutions Ltd.

Executive Summary
This report analyses the current mobile app user acquisition landscape and proposes a strategic approach to increase user acquisition for TechBridge Solutions' flagship app, *Connect+*. The report identifies key target audiences, outlines effective marketing channels, and recommends performance metrics for tracking campaign success.

Introduction
In today's competitive app market, acquiring new users is crucial for the growth and success of TechBridge Solutions. This report examines the current user acquisition strategy, identifies areas for improvement, and presents a comprehensive plan to drive user growth.

Competitive Analysis
A thorough analysis of competitor apps in the same category will be conducted to identify their user acquisition tactics, strengths, and weaknesses.

Target Audience Segmentation
Detailed segmentation of the target audience based on demographics, interests, and behaviour will be carried out to tailor marketing efforts effectively.

User Acquisition Channels

- **Organic Growth**: Optimise app store optimisation (ASO) to improve app visibility.

- **Paid Advertising**: Utilise platforms like Google Ads, Facebook Ads, and Apple Search Ads to reach a wider audience.

- **Social Media Marketing**: Leverage social media platforms to engage with potential users and drive app downloads.

- **Influencer Partnerships**: Collaborate with relevant influencers to promote the app to their audience.

- **Referral Programs**: Implement a referral programme to encourage existing users to invite friends.

Marketing Campaign Development

Create compelling marketing campaigns aligned with the target audience, highlighting the app's unique value proposition.

Performance Metrics

Define key performance indicators (KPIs) to measure the success of user acquisition campaigns, including:

- Cost per acquisition (CPA)

- Return on investment (ROI)

- User retention rate

- App store ratings and reviews

Conclusion

By implementing a comprehensive user acquisition strategy, TechBridge Solutions can significantly increase app downloads, improve user engagement, and drive overall business growth.

Recommendations

- Conduct regular A/B testing to optimise marketing campaigns.

- Monitor industry trends and adjust the strategy accordingly.

- Invest in data analytics to gain valuable insights into user behaviour.

Proposal: Cloud Migration Project
TechBridge Solutions Ltd.

Executive Summary

This proposal outlines a strategic plan to migrate TechBridge Solutions' IT infrastructure to a cloud-based environment. By leveraging cloud technology, the company can enhance scalability, reduce costs, and improve operational efficiency.

Problem Statement

The current on-premises IT infrastructure faces limitations in scalability, flexibility, and cost-effectiveness. A cloud migration is necessary to address these challenges and support future growth.

Proposed Solution

- **Cloud Platform Selection**: Evaluate and select the most suitable cloud platform (e.g., AWS, Azure, GCP) based on business requirements and cost considerations.

- **Data Migration Planning**: Develop a comprehensive data migration strategy, including data assessment, migration tools, and testing.

- **Infrastructure and Application Migration**: Migrate servers, applications, and databases to the cloud environment.

- **Security and Compliance**: Implement robust security measures to protect sensitive data and ensure compliance with industry regulations.

- **Change Management**: Develop a communication and training plan for employees to facilitate a smooth transition.

Budget

A detailed budget allocation for cloud services, migration costs, and ongoing operational expenses will be provided.

Timeline

A project timeline with key milestones and deliverables will be outlined.

Evaluation Plan

Key performance indicators (KPIs) will be defined to measure the success of the cloud migration project, including cost savings, performance improvement, and security compliance

How to Adapt Your Writing Style to Different Audiences (Formal, Informal)

One of the keys to effective written communication is knowing your audience and tailoring your tone to fit them. Your writing style should shift depending on whether you are addressing a senior executive, a colleague, or a close friend.

Formal Writing: Formal writing is used in business reports, professional emails, or any situation where you need to maintain a certain level of respect and professionalism. This involves using full sentences, formal greetings, and proper titles. For example, if you are writing to a client or your boss, you would say, "Dear Mr. Ajayi, I hope this message finds you well," instead of, "Hi Ajayi, hope you're good." The formality of your writing shows that you take the interaction seriously.

- **To:** [email address removed]

- **From:** [email address removed]

- **Subject:** Enquiry about Waste Management Services

Dear Sir/Madam,

I hope this email finds you well.

I am writing to inquire about the waste management services provided by Lagos State Waste Management Authority (LAWMA) for residential areas. I reside at 23, Adebayo Street, Surulere, Lagos.

Could you please provide me with the procedures for registering for waste collection services, as well as the associated fees? I would also appreciate it if you could inform me of the waste collection schedule for the Surulere area.

Thank you very much for your prompt attention to this matter.

Kind regards,
Adebayo Olowo

This formal email uses a respectful greeting, full sentences, and polite language.

Informal Email: On the other hand, informal writing can be used with colleagues you are familiar with or even friends at work. The tone is more relaxed, but it should still be respectful. For instance, if you are emailing a colleague you work closely with, you might say, "Hey Tunde, just a quick reminder about the meeting tomorrow." It is friendly and approachable without being too casual. An example is written below.

- **To:** [email address removed]

- **From:** [email address removed]

- **Subject:** Weekend Plans?

Hi Chike,

Hope you're doing well.

Are you free this weekend? I'm thinking of heading to Lekki Phase 1 to check out that new suya spot I heard about. It could be fun to hang out, grab a bite, and maybe catch a movie afterwards.

Let me know if you're up for it.

Cheers,
Adaobi

Example 3: Email with Bullet Points

- **To:** [email address removed]

- **From:** [email address removed]

- **Subject:** Interest in Techpoint Startup Bootcamp

Dear Techpoint Team,

I trust this email finds you well.

I am writing to express my keen interest in the Techpoint Startup Bootcamp. I am particularly eager to participate in the digital marketing and product development modules.

Attached is my CV for your review.

Here's a brief overview of my skills:

- *Strong background in digital marketing, with experience in SEO, social media, and content creation.*
- *Proficient in using digital marketing tools such as Google Analytics and Hootsuite.*
- *Passionate about technology and entrepreneurship.*

I look forward to hearing from you soon.

Thank you for your consideration.

Best regards,
Girl's mind

Formal vs. Informal Tone

Example 1: Formal Tone

Dear Mr Adebayo,

I hope you are well.

I am writing to formally request a meeting to discuss the proposed partnership between our companies. As previously mentioned, we believe there is significant potential for collaboration in the renewable energy sector.

I am available to meet on the 15th or 16th of March. Kindly let me know if either of these dates suits you, or if another time would be more convenient.

Thank you for your time and consideration.

Sincerely,
Good luck Okoro

Example 2: Informal Tone

Hi Bola,

It's been a while! How have you been?

I hope you're doing great. I'm planning a small get-together at my place next Saturday, and it would be lovely to catch up.

Let me know if you can make it.

Best,
Skin

Example 3: Tone Mismatch

Avoid this type of email

Dear Sir/Madam,

Hi there! I hope you're well. I'm writing to ask about the possibility of an internship position at your company.

I'm really interested in working at [Company Name] because of the amazing work you do in [industry].

Looking forward to your reply!

Best regards,
Indeed

Business Letters

Example 1: Enquiry Letter

Mr Adewale Ojo
Managing Director
Greenville Farms Ltd.
12, Obafemi Awolowo Way
Ikeja, Lagos

15th March, 2024

Dear Mr Ojo,

I trust this letter finds you well.

I am writing to inquire about the possibility of becoming a distributor for Greenville Farms' agricultural products in the Enugu region. My company, Umunna Enterprises, has a strong distribution network in the Southeast, and we believe there is significant market potential for your products in this area.

We would appreciate it if you could provide us with information regarding your distributor programme, including product availability, pricing, and delivery terms.

We look forward to the possibility of a mutually beneficial partnership.

Yours sincerely,
Chidi Brothers

Example 2: Complaint Letter

Mr Peter Adeyemi
Customer Service Manager
Zenith Bank Plc.
Victoria Island, Lagos

18th April, 2024

Dear Mr Adeyemi,

I hope you are well.

I am writing to formally lodge a complaint regarding an unauthorised withdrawal of N50,000 from my Zenith Bank account on the 15th of April, 2024. My account number is 1234567890.

I have contacted my bank branch, and they advised me to submit a formal complaint in writing. I have attached a copy of my account statement for your reference.

I kindly request that the unauthorised withdrawal be reversed and the amount credited back to my account as soon as possible.

I look forward to a prompt resolution to this matter.

Yours faithfully,
Ngozi Okoro

Example 3: Cover Letter

Mr Adewale Ojo
Human Resources Manager

First Bank of Nigeria Plc.
Marina, Lagos

22nd May, 2024

Dear Mr Ojo,

I hope you are well.

I am writing to express my strong interest in the Marketing Officer position advertised on your company's website. I have been following First Bank's innovative marketing campaigns and am greatly impressed by your commitment to excellence.

With a Bachelor's degree in Marketing from the University of Lagos and three years of experience in the banking industry, I am confident in my ability to make a significant contribution to your team. I possess strong analytical and communication skills and am proficient in using digital marketing tools.

I have attached my CV for your review, which provides further details about my qualifications and experience.

Thank you for considering my application. I look forward to the opportunity to discuss my candidacy further in an interview.

Yours sincerely,
Tope Adebayo

Basic Email Etiquette and Tips

1. **Choose a Professional Email Address**

   Make sure your email address looks professional, ideally using your name. Avoid using nicknames or anything that might seem unprofessional.

2. **Craft a Clear Subject Line**

   The subject line should be straightforward and let the recipient know what to expect. For instance, *"Request for Meeting: Project Review – 15th August 2024."*

3. **Begin with a Polite Greeting**

   Use a respectful salutation, such as *"Dear Mr. Adeyemi,"* or *"Hello Dr. Okon,"* depending on how well you know the recipient.

4. **Keep It Brief and Focused**

   Get straight to the point and avoid unnecessary details. For example, rather than saying, *"I hope this email finds you well. I wanted to touch base about the upcoming meeting and cover a few important topics,"* you might say, *"I'd like to discuss the agenda for our upcoming meeting."*

5. **Mind Your Tone**

   It is easy for emails to be misunderstood, so choose your words carefully. Avoid using all caps, which can come across as shouting. Polite phrases like *"please"* and *"thank you"* can help set the right tone.

6. **Check Your Grammar and Spelling**

   Take a moment to proofread your email before hitting send. Ensure your sentences are complete, and your punctuation is correct.

7. **Avoid Abbreviations and Emojis**

   Unless it is an informal conversation, steer clear of abbreviations like "u" for "you" and avoid using emojis.

8. **Use Paragraphs and Formatting**

   Break up your text into paragraphs for easier reading. If you are listing items, bullet points or numbering can make your email clearer.

9. **Attach Files Correctly**

   Double-check that you've attached the right documents, and mention them in your email. For example, *"Please find the report attached."*

10. **End with a Polite Sign-Off**

    Close your email with a courteous sign-off, such as *"Best regards,"* *"Sincerely,"* or *"Kind regards,"* followed by your name.

11. Respond in a Timely Manner

Aim to reply to emails within 24-48 hours. If you need more time, send a quick acknowledgement and let them know when you will follow up properly.

12. Be Careful with "Reply All"

Only use "Reply All" if everyone needs to see your response. Otherwise, just reply to the sender.

13. Use CC and BCC Thoughtfully

CC (carbon copy) those who need to stay informed but are not the main recipients. BCC (blind carbon copy) is useful for keeping email addresses private or avoiding cluttering inboxes with a long list of recipients.

14. Consider When You Send Your Email

Try not to send emails late at night or over the weekend unless it is urgent. If needed, you can schedule the email to be sent during regular working hours.

15. Include a Signature

Add a signature with your full name, job title, company, and contact details, so it is easy for the recipient to get in touch with you.

16. Follow Up Politely

If you have not heard back in a reasonable amount of time, send a gentle reminder. For example, *"I'm just following up on my previous email regarding [subject]. Please let me know if you require any further information."*

CHAPTER 6

WORKPLACE ETIQUETTE

Workplace etiquette is essential for a professional and respectful environment. In this chapter, we focus on two key areas: *Customer Service* and *Why Compliments on Appearance Do Not Belong in the Workplace and Customer Service.* The first section discusses how treating customers with respect and attentiveness builds trust and loyalty. The second addresses why appearance-based compliments can feel personal or uncomfortable, emphasising the importance of professionalism in interactions. Let us consider these areas.

Why Compliments on Appearance Don't Belong in the Workplace

A few years ago, a close friend of mine, who had left Nigeria for the UK, and worked at a tech company in Bristol, told me about a well-meaning compliment he gave a female colleague on how "stunning" she looked during a meeting. He also tried being flowery by commenting on her shapely figure. What he thought was harmless left her feeling uneasy and distracted. Soon after, she mentioned it to HR, and it spiralled into a bigger issue, creating tension in the office. This situation could have been easily avoided if he had focused on her brilliant presentation instead.

Rhonda Harvill sued her employer, Westward Communications, in 2006, after enduring months of inappropriate comments and physical advances from a male supervisor. The comments included remarks about her appearance and body, making her workplace environment hostile and unbearable. The U.S. Court of Appeals for the Fifth Circuit found that Harvill had been subjected to sexual harassment, ruling that such comments and actions created a hostile work environment. The case is

often cited as an example of how persistent, unwanted comments about appearance can lead to legal action and employer liability.

In 2010, in the United States of America, a female TSA (Transportation Security Administration) employee, Jane Greenwood, filed a lawsuit claiming that her supervisor frequently commented on her appearance and made remarks about her body. These comments made her feel uncomfortable and objectified, ultimately leading her to file a sexual harassment claim.The case resulted in a substantial financial settlement for Greenwood, along with a court order requiring the TSA to improve its policies on workplace harassment. This case is a key example of how appearance-based comments can lead to successful legal claims for sexual harassment.

These cases just prove that in the workplace, commenting on a woman's beauty or body parts is often seen as inappropriate, and for good reason. Here's why it's best to steer clear of such remarks:

Keeping it Professional: Work is about what you bring to the table—your skills, your ideas, your contributions. When compliments veer into personal appearance, it can distract from the real focus: your professional value. Instead of acknowledging her achievements, you risk making her feel like her looks are what matter most, which is not what any of us are there for.

Power Dynamics and Perception: Even if you think your comment is harmless or well-meaning, it can easily be misinterpreted. In a professional setting, especially where there's a hierarchy, these remarks can come off as patronising or even as a power play. The last thing anyone wants is to make a colleague feel uncomfortable or question your intentions.

Respecting Boundaries: Clear boundaries are essential at work. Compliments about appearance can blur those lines, leading to awkward situations or, in worst cases, accusations of harassment. It's better to keep things straightforward and respectful by focusing on what's relevant to the job.

Promoting Inclusivity and Respect: When we focus too much on looks, we risk creating an environment where people feel judged on their appearance rather than their work. This can alienate colleagues and make them feel

less valued. Praising someone's creativity, work ethic, or problem-solving skills is a more respectful and inclusive approach that everyone can appreciate.

What You Can Say Instead

You can comment on their work ethic and diligence with the following:

- *"You're like a machine—always working hard and staying on top of things."*
- *"Your commitment really inspires the rest of us to keep pushing."*
- *"The amount of effort you put in doesn't go unnoticed. We all appreciate it."*

When it comes to a colleague's skills and expertise, you might say the following:

- *"When it comes to this, you make it look easy because you're that good."*
- *"You've got a real knack for this. It's clear you know your stuff."*
- *"You're the go-to person for this kind of work for a reason."*

Are they creative and innovative? Say the following:

- *"You've got such a unique way of thinking; it always brings fresh ideas."*
- *"Your creativity really brought a spark to this project."*
- *"I love how you always come up with something different and exciting."*

Does your colleague possess great leadership and Teamwork skills? These will help:

- *"You have a natural way of making everyone feel included and valued."*
- *"Your leadership makes it easy for the team to stay motivated."*
- *"You're great at bringing out the best in everyone."*

If they are good at solving problems, say the following:

- *"You always find a way to make things work, no matter how tricky."*
- *"You've got a real talent for turning challenges into opportunities."*
- *"Your decisions are always so well thought out—it's impressive."*

If they have great communication and presentation skills, you might consider saying the following:

- *"You have a way of making things clear and easy to understand."*
- *"The way you explained that was spot on—everyone got it right away."*
- *"You really know how to keep people engaged when you speak."*

If they are reliable and accountable, you might say the following:

- *"It's reassuring to know I can always count on you to get things done."*
- *"You never drop the ball, and that's something everyone appreciates."*
- *"You're the kind of person who follows through, no matter what."*

What to do When Gathering Your Thoughts

Taking a moment to gather your thoughts before responding is crucial, especially in professional settings. It allows you to provide a thoughtful and well-considered answer. Instead of staying quiet during conversations, use these phrases and strategies to help you gain thinking time and ensure your responses are clear and effective.

Phrases to Buy Time

When faced with a question or situation that requires a moment of reflection, you can use various phrases to give yourself the time you need:

Acknowledging the Question:

- *"That's a great question. Let me think about it for a moment."*
- *"Interesting point. I need a second to consider it."*

Direct Requests:

- *"Could you please give me a moment to think about that?"*
- *"I'd like to take a few seconds to consider my response."*
- *"Let me think about that for a moment."*

Clarifying the Question:

- *"Just to make sure I understand, are you asking about...?"*
- *"Could you please elaborate on that?"*

Repeating the Question:

- *"So, you're asking if...?"*
- *"If I understand correctly, you want to know...?"*

Using Fillers:

- *"Well, let's see..."*
- *"Hmm, that's something to think about..."*

Strategies for Effective Thinking Time

To make the most of your thinking time, you can employ several strategies:

Pause and Breathe:

Take a deep breath before responding. This helps you gather your thoughts and calm any nerves.

Organise Your Thoughts:

Mentally outline key points or arguments you want to make before speaking.

Paraphrase the Question:

Restate the question in your own words. This not only buys you time but also ensures you understand the question correctly.

Consider Different Perspectives:

Explore various viewpoints to gain a broader understanding of the situation.

Ask for Clarification:

If the question is unclear, ask for more details. This can give you additional time to think.

Use Transitional Phrases:

Phrases like *"That's an interesting perspective"* or *"I haven't thought about it that way before"* can give you a moment to formulate your response.

Acknowledge the Complexity:

"That's a complex issue. Let me take a moment to think about it."

Break Down the Answer:

Start by addressing one part of the question, which can give you more time to think about the rest.

Additional Tips

Be genuine: Avoid overusing these phrases, as it may compromise your credibility.

Practice: The more you practise, the more natural these phrases will become.

Adapt to the situation: Choose phrases and strategies that are appropriate for the context.

Remember: Thinking time is not about avoiding a question but about providing a thoughtful and well-considered response.

Example in Practice

Question: "What are your thoughts on the new marketing strategy?"

Response: "That's a great question. Let me think about it for a moment. If I understand correctly, you're asking about the potential impact of the new strategy on our current market position. Well, let's see... I believe there are several factors to consider..."

Customer Service

If you want to build strong relationships with clients and ensure that they are satisfied, consider providing excellent customer service. Here are the three key components of outstanding customer service, along with practical examples and key phrases that can help in various situations.

1. Empathy and Understanding

According to the Cambridge English dictionary, empathy is defined as the ability to share someone else's feelings or experiences by imagining what it would be like to be in that person's situation. How can empathy be applied in customer service?

- **Active Listening**: If a customer is upset about a delayed shipment, it's crucial to listen without interrupting. You might respond, "I understand that your shipment was delayed, and I can see how that would be frustrating. Let me check the status for you and find a solution."

- **Emotional Intelligence**: Pay attention to the customer's tone and body language. If they seem exasperated, acknowledge their feelings with something like, "I can understand how frustrating this must be."

- **Perspective-Taking**: Put yourself in the customer's shoes. If a product arrives damaged, you could say, "I'm really sorry to hear that your product arrived damaged. I understand how disappointing that must be. Let's get this sorted out for you right away."

2. Efficiency and Responsiveness

Being prompt and efficient in addressing customer issues shows that you value their time and are committed to resolving their problems.

- **Quick Response Times**: If a customer emails about a billing error, a prompt reply like, "Thank you for bringing this to our attention. We are currently reviewing your account and will update you within the next 24 hours," demonstrates efficiency.

- **Problem-Solving**: When a customer reports a software bug, quickly identifying the issue and providing a temporary workaround, such as, "We've identified the issue and are working on a fix. In the meantime, you can use this workaround to continue your work," can be very reassuring.

- **Follow-Through**: After resolving a product defect, it's important to follow up with the customer. You might say, "I wanted to check in and

make sure everything is working smoothly with your subscription. Is there anything else I can assist you with?"

3. **Proactivity and Personalisation**

Anticipating customer needs and providing personalised service makes customers feel valued and appreciated.

- **Anticipating Needs**: If a customer frequently purchases skincare products, you could suggest a subscription service to ensure they never run out. This proactive approach shows you're thinking ahead.

- **Personalised Service**: Remembering a customer's name and past purchases can go a long way. For example, "Hello, Mr. Johnson! I see you usually order the premium vitamin c serum. Would you like to add that to your order today?" shows attention to detail.

- **Going the Extra Mile**: If a customer is looking for a specific product that's out of stock, don't leave them just like that; you might find a similar item and offer a discount, saying, "While the item you wanted is out of stock, we have a similar product available. As an apology for the inconvenience, we'd like to offer you a 10% discount on your purchase."

Key Phrases for Customer Service

1. **Greeting and Establishing Rapport:**

    Scenario: A customer calls about a product issue.

    Phrase: "Good morning/afternoon. Thank you for contacting [Company Name]. How can I help you today?"

2. **Active Listening and Empathy**:

    Scenario: A customer is upset about a long wait time.

    Phrase: "I understand you're frustrated with the wait time. Let me apologise for the inconvenience."

3. **Problem-Solving and Resolution**:

Scenario: A customer's order is incorrect.

Phrase: "I apologise for the error. Let's get that sorted out right away. I can arrange a replacement or refund."

4. **Building Customer Loyalty**:

Scenario: A customer compliments your service.

Phrase: "Thank you for your kind words. We appreciate your business and value your loyalty."

5. **Clarifying and Confirming**:

Scenario: A customer asks about multiple features of a product.

Phrase: "Just to confirm, you're asking about the warranty and the return policy, correct?"

6. **Apologising**:

Scenario: A customer received the wrong order.

Phrase: "I apologise for the inconvenience. Let's get this corrected for you right away."

7. **Thanking and Appreciating**:

Scenario: A customer provides feedback on a product.

Phrase: "Thank you for bringing this to our attention. We appreciate your feedback."

8. **Closing the Conversation**:

Scenario: After resolving a customer's issue.

Phrase: "Is there anything else I can assist you with? Thank you for contacting us. Have a great day!"

Dealing with Upset Customers

Scenario: A customer at a Lagos phone store is upset because their newly purchased phone isn't working.

Steps:

1. **Listen:** Allow the customer to express their frustration without interruption. For example, "I understand you're upset about the phone issue."

2. **Show Empathy:** Acknowledge their feelings. "I can see how this situation is frustrating for you."

3. **Apologise Sincerely:** Even if it's not your fault, apologise for the inconvenience. "I'm really sorry for the trouble this has caused you."

4. **Offer a Solution:** Provide a practical solution, such as a replacement or repair. "We can replace the phone for you or have it repaired immediately."

5. **Follow Up:** Ensure the issue is resolved to the customer's satisfaction. "I'll check back with you in a few days to make sure everything is working fine."

Making Polite Requests

Scenario: Asking a colleague to help with a project at an office in Abuja.

Steps:

Use Polite Language: Requesting Assistance:

- *"Would you be so kind as to assist me with this task?"*
- *"Could I trouble you for a moment of your time?"*

Seeking Permission:

- *"Would it be possible for me to leave a bit early today?"*
- *"May I have your approval to proceed with this plan?"*

Offering Help:

- *"If you need any help, please don't hesitate to ask."*
- *"I would be happy to assist you with that."*

Be Specific

Giving Instructions:

- *"Please review the attached document and provide your feedback by Friday."*
- *"Could you prepare a summary of the meeting notes and email it to the team by noon tomorrow?"*

Making Requests:

- *"Could you please draft the quarterly report and include the sales data from January to March?"*
- *"Please schedule a meeting with the marketing team for Thursday at 2 PM."*

Providing Information:

- *"The project deadline is on the 15th of August, so we need the final draft by the 10th."*
- *"Our target audience for this campaign is young professionals aged 25 to 35."*

Show Appreciation

Thanking Someone:

- *"Thank you very much for your prompt response."*
- *"I really appreciate your help with the project."*
- *"Thank you."*

Recognising Efforts:

- *"Your hard work and dedication are greatly appreciated."*
- *"Thank you for going above and beyond to ensure the project's success."*

Expressing Gratitude:

- *"I'm grateful for your assistance with this matter."*
- *"We appreciate your continued support and partnership."*

CHAPTER 7

GRAMMAR

The *Grammar* section sheds light on some of the most commonly misused expressions among Nigerian speakers. Here, we will address these frequent errors in a practical and relatable way, exploring why they occur and offering simple, memorable corrections. The goal is to help you communicate with clarity and confidence, avoiding misunderstandings and strengthening your command of English.

Commonly Misused Expressions by Nigerian Speakers

Incorrect: "12 AM midnight"
Correct: "Midnight"
Reason: "AM" is redundant since midnight itself is unambiguous.

Example: "The system will be updated at midnight."

Incorrect: "Transport fare"
Correct: "Fare"
Reason: "Fare" is the money that you pay for a journey in a vehicle."

Example: "Bus fares are going up again."

Incorrect: "Absolutely essential"

Correct: "Essential"

Reason: "Absolutely" is redundant because essential means absolutely necessary.

Example: "Having a clear strategy is essential."

Good in vs. Good at

Incorrect: good in
Correct: good at

Reason: "Good at" is the appropriate preposition used to describe proficiency or skill in a particular area, whereas "good in" is not conventionally used in this context.

Example: She is good at mathematics.

I appreciate

Incorrect: I appreciate

Correct: I appreciate it/this/that/you.

Reason: "Appreciate" is a transitive verb, meaning it requires an object to complete the sentence; without an object, the sentence is incomplete.

Example: I appreciate your help with the project.

Discuss about something

Incorrect: discuss about something

Correct: discuss something

Reason: The verb "discuss" does not require the preposition "about." It directly takes its object.

Example: Let us discuss the plans for the event.

Like a log of wood

Incorrect: like a log of wood

Correct: like a log

Reason: The phrase "like a log" is the correct idiomatic expression, indicating someone is completely still or unresponsive.

Example: He slept like a log last night.

Write the examination

Incorrect: write the examination

Correct: sit (for)/take/do the examination.

Reason: "Sit for," "take," or "do" are the correct verbs used to indicate participating in an exam.

Example: She will take the examination tomorrow.

On a single file

Incorrect: on a single file

Correct: in single file

Reason: "In single file" is the correct expression that describes people walking one behind the other, while "on a single file" is not grammatically correct.

Example: The children walked to the assembly hall in single file.

Swear for you

Incorrect: swear for you

Correct: swear at you

Reason: "Swear for" suggests making an oath on someone's behalf, while "swear at" means to verbally attack or insult someone.

Example: He swore at me when I made the mistake.

Most proudest person

Incorrect: most proudest person

Correct: the proudest person

Reason: "Proudest" already conveys the superlative form, so adding "most" is redundant.

Example: She is the proudest person in the room.

Put to bed

Incorrect: put to bed

Correct: give birth to

Reason: "Put to bed" refers to putting someone to sleep, whereas "give birth to" is the correct term for the act of delivering a baby.

Example: She gave birth to a beautiful baby girl.

On the fast lane

Incorrect: on the fast lane

Correct: in the fast lane

Reason: The phrase "in the fast lane" is used to describe someone living a fast-paced life or pursuing an exciting lifestyle.

Example: He enjoys living in the fast lane.

April Fool

Incorrect: April Fool

Correct: April Fool's Day

Reason: The correct term is "April Fool's Day," referring to the day dedicated to pranks and jokes.

Example: We always play tricks on April Fool's Day.

Burn the midnight candle

Incorrect: burn the midnight candle

Correct: burn the midnight oil

Reason: The expression is "burn the midnight oil," which means to stay up late working or studying.

Example: I had to burn the midnight oil to finish my report.

Master of ceremony

Incorrect: master of ceremony

Correct: master of ceremonies

Reason: The correct term is "master of ceremonies," referring to a person who hosts an event or ceremony.

Example: The master of ceremonies introduced the speakers at the event.

A slip of tongue

Incorrect: a slip of tongue

Correct: a slip of the tongue

Reason: The correct expression is "a slip of the tongue," which refers to a mistake made in speech.

Example: I made a slip of the tongue when I called him by the wrong name.

Turn back the hand of time

Incorrect: turn back the hand of time

Correct: turn back the clock

Reason: The idiomatic expression is "turn back the clock," meaning to return to an earlier time or situation.

Example: Sometimes, I wish I could turn back the clock to my childhood.

A goal-getter

Incorrect: a goal-getter

Correct: a go-getter

Reason: The correct term is "go-getter," referring to someone who is ambitious and proactive in pursuing their goals.

Example: As a go-getter, she always seeks new opportunities for success.

Sprays

Incorrect: sprays

Correct: perfumes

Reason: While "sprays" can refer to aerosol products, "perfumes" specifically denote scented liquids.

Example: I bought several new perfumes for the upcoming party.

Godsent

Incorrect: godsent

Correct: godsend

Reason: The correct term is "godsend," meaning something or someone that comes at the right moment, often unexpectedly.

Example: The extra help during the busy season was a real godsend.

Running nose

Incorrect: running nose

Correct: runny nose

Reason: The correct expression is "runny nose," which describes a nose that is discharging mucus.

Example: He has a runny nose because of the cold weather.

Fight fire for fire

Incorrect: fight fire for fire

Correct: fight fire with fire

Reason: The correct idiom is "fight fire with fire," meaning to respond to an attack with a similar attack.

Example: She decided to fight fire with fire and defend her position aggressively.

Fruit of labour

Incorrect: fruit of labour

Correct: fruits of labour

Reason: The expression should be "fruits of labour," as it refers to the various results or rewards from hard work.

Example: The fruits of their labour were evident in the successful project.

Next week Sunday

Incorrect: next week Sunday

Correct: next Sunday

Reason: The correct expression is "next Sunday," which refers to the Sunday that follows the current week.

Example: We will have a family gathering next Sunday.

Tosin comes back in the night

Incorrect: Tosin comes back in the night

Correct: Tosin comes back at night

Reason: "At night" refers to a regular occurrence, making it suitable for the present tense "comes." "In the night" is more appropriate for a specific event that happened in the past.

Example: Tosin comes back at night every day.

Sleep off vs. Sleep

Incorrect: sleep off

Correct: sleep

Reason: "Sleep off" specifically means to recover from something, like a hangover, by sleeping. It does not apply to general sleeping.

Example: I need to sleep for a few hours to feel refreshed.

Yesterday night

Incorrect: yesterday night

Correct: last night

Reason: While "yesterday morning," "yesterday afternoon," and "yesterday evening" are acceptable, "yesterday night" is not used in standard English; "last night" is preferred.

Example: We watched a movie last night.

Is equals to

Incorrect: is equals to

Correct: is equal to

Reason: The correct phrase is "is equal to," which denotes equivalence. "Equals" is not used in this context.

Example: Ten plus five is equal to fifteen.

Vacate

Incorrect: vacate

Correct: holiday

Reason: "Vacate" means to leave or empty a place, which does not fit the context of a school break. In British English, "holiday" is used, while in American English, it is referred to as "vacation."

Example: The students will have a holiday next week.

Poke nose into

Incorrect: poke nose into

Correct: poke (one's) nose

Reason: The correct expression is "poke (one's) nose," which means to interfere in someone else's affairs.

Example: She likes to poke her nose into other people's business.

Wrestle power

Incorrect: wrestle power

Correct: wrest power

Reason: "Wrest" is the appropriate verb for taking something with effort, while "wrestle" implies physical combat, which is not applicable here.

Example: They attempted to wrest power from the ruling party.

On my laps

Incorrect: on my laps

Correct: on my lap

Reason: The correct phrase is "on my lap," which refers to the area between the waist and the knees when sitting. "Laps" is incorrect in this context.

Example: The cat is sitting on my lap.

Raining season

Incorrect: raining season

Correct: rainy season

Reason: The correct expression is "rainy season," which describes the time of year when it frequently rains.

Example: The rainy season typically starts in June.

Making noise

Incorrect: making noise

Correct: making a noise

Reason: The expression "making a noise" is correct when referring to producing sound, while "making noise" is more informal and can imply creating a disturbance.

Example: The children are making a noise in the garden.

Empty barrels make the loudest noise

Incorrect: Empty barrels make the loudest noise

Correct: Empty vessels make the most noise

Reason: The standard term in the idiom is "vessels," while "barrels" is a non-standard substitution.

Example: As they say, empty vessels make the most noise in meetings.

Lick an orange

Incorrect: lick an orange

Correct: eat an orange

Reason: The phrase "lick an orange" does not convey the intended action of consuming the fruit; "eat" is the correct verb.

Example: I like to eat an orange as a healthy snack.

A good news

Incorrect: a good news

Correct: good news

Reason: "News" is an uncountable noun, so it should not be preceded by "a."

Example: I have good news to share with you.

Raise an alarm

Incorrect: raise an alarm

Correct: raise the alarm

Reason: The correct phrase is "raise the alarm," which means to alert others about a danger.

Example: She raised the alarm when she saw the fire

A Vast Majority Of

Incorrect: A vast majority of

Correct: The vast majority of

Reason: "The vast majority of" is the correct expression, as "the" specifies the majority being referred to.

Example: The vast majority of students attended the lecture.

Any Moment from Now

Incorrect: any moment from now

Correct: any moment now / at any moment

Reason: "Any moment from now" is redundant. "Any moment now" or "at any moment" are the correct forms.

Example: The guests will arrive any moment now.

Pot Belly

Incorrect: pot belly

Correct: a pot belly / a pot-bellied man

Reason: "Pot belly" should either have an article or be used as an adjective (pot-bellied). It can also be written as "potbelly."

Example: He has a pot belly from lack of exercise.

Make a Complain

Incorrect: make a complain

Correct: make a complaint

Reason: "Complaint" is the noun form, while "complain" is the verb form.

Example: I made a complaint to customer service.

Last But Not the Least

Incorrect: last but not the least

Correct: last but not least

Reason: "Last but not least" is the correct expression for emphasising the importance of the final item.

Example: Last but not least, I want to thank everyone for their support.

Cut Your Coat According to Your Size

Incorrect: cut your coat according to your size

Correct: cut your coat according to your cloth / cut your cloth according to your means

Reason: The correct idiom advises acting within one's resources, so "cloth" or "means" is more appropriate.

Example: You should cut your coat according to your cloth and avoid unnecessary expenses.

As At When Necessary

Incorrect: as at when necessary

Correct: as and when necessary

Reason: "As and when necessary" is the correct expression to indicate doing something only when needed.

Example: The document will be reviewed as and when necessary.

Stay on the Queue

Incorrect: stay on the queue

Correct: wait in the queue

Reason: The correct preposition is "in" the queue, meaning to line up for something.

Example: Please wait in the queue for your turn.

Wait for Your Turn

Incorrect: wait for your turn

Correct: wait your turn

Reason: The concise expression "wait your turn" is correct and commonly used.

Example: You must wait your turn before speaking.

Born with a Silver Spoon

Incorrect: born with a silver spoon

Correct: born with a silver spoon in his/her mouth

Reason: The full expression "born with a silver spoon in one's mouth" specifies being born into wealth.

Example: She was born with a silver spoon in her mouth.

Emphasised On

Incorrect: emphasised on

Correct: emphasised the

Reason: "Emphasised" is a transitive verb and should directly follow the object, such as "the importance."

Example: She emphasised the need for punctuality.

Beauty Lies in the Eyes of the Beholder

Incorrect: beauty lies in the eyes of the beholder

Correct: beauty is in the eye of the beholder

Reason: The correct expression is "beauty is in the eye of the beholder," implying that beauty is subjective.

Example: Beauty is in the eye of the beholder.

In the Agenda

Incorrect: in the agenda

Correct: on the agenda

Reason: "On the agenda" is correct; "in" is not a suitable collocate with "agenda."

Example: The budget proposal is the first item on the agenda.

Whereabout Is

Incorrect: whereabout is

Correct: whereabouts is/are

Reason: "Whereabouts" is the correct term for referring to someone's location, and it can take singular or plural verbs.

Example: His whereabouts are currently unknown.

Let Bygone Be Bygone

Incorrect: let bygone be bygone / let bygones be bygone

Correct: let bygones be bygones

Reason: The phrase "let bygones be bygones" is used to suggest letting past grievances go.

Example: Let bygones be bygones and move forward together.

Double Dating vs. Two-Timing

Incorrect: double dating

Correct: two-timing

Reason: "Two-timing" implies being deceitful with two partners, while "double dating" refers to going out with two couples.

Example: She caught him two-timing her with another woman.

Chat You Up

Incorrect: chat you up

Correct: chat to you / chat with you

Reason: "Chat you up" can imply flirtation, while "chat to" or "chat with" is more neutral.

Example: I wanted to chat with you about the event.

People from All Works of Life

Incorrect: people from all works of life

Correct: people from all walks of life

Reason: "Walks of life" is the correct expression, referring to diverse backgrounds.

Example: Our team includes people from all walks of life.

The Shirt is Bogus

Incorrect: the shirt is bogus

Correct: the shirt is oversized / too big

Reason: "Bogus" means fake, so it does not describe fit or size. "Oversized" or "too big" is more suitable.

Example: The shirt is too big for him.

Jeans Is

Incorrect: jeans is

Correct: these jeans are / this pair of jeans is

Reason: "Jeans" is treated as plural, so it requires a plural verb, or "pair" can be used with a singular verb.

Example: These jeans are very comfortable.

In the Television

Incorrect: in the television

Correct: on the television

Reason: "On the television" is correct when referring to what's being broadcast.

Example: There is a good show on the television tonight.

An Information

Incorrect: an information

Correct: a piece/bit of information / information

Reason: "Information" is uncountable, so "an" should not precede it; use "a piece of information" for specific details.

Example: I received an important piece of information.

Know (One's) Onion

Incorrect: know (one's) onion

Correct: know (one's) onions / know one's stuff

Reason: The expression "know one's onions" or "know one's stuff" implies being knowledgeable or skilled.

Example: He really knows his onions when it comes to accounting.

A Matured Person

Incorrect: she married a matured man

Correct: she married a mature man

Reason: "Matured" is not the correct adjective here; "mature" is the suitable form.

Example: She married a mature man who is very responsible.

Materials

Incorrect: materials

Correct: material

Reason: "Material" is uncountable in this context and does not take an "s" in singular use.

Example: I am gathering material for my next article.

Human Resource Department

Incorrect: human resource department

Correct: human resources / personnel department

Reason: "Human resources" or simply "personnel" are the correct terms for this department.

Example: She works in the human resources department.

Above or Over?

- **Above (preposition/adverb):** Higher than something else but not directly touching it.

- **Over (preposition/adverb):** Directly upward and often covering or crossing something.

  Usage:

  "Above" is used when something is not touching the other object: The ceiling fan is above the table.

  "Over" is used when something is covering or crossing something: I spread the cloth over the table.

  Example Sentences:

The plane flew above Lagos.

The rain poured over the entire city.

Across, Over or Through?

- **Across (preposition/adverb):** From one side to the other.
- **Over (preposition/adverb):** On the other side of something high, like a mountain.
- **Through (preposition/adverb):** From one side of an enclosed space to the other.

  Usage:

  "Across" refers to a flat surface: I walked across the road.

  "Over" refers to something elevated: We went over the bridge.

  "Through" refers to passing inside something: We drove through the tunnel.

  Example Sentences:

  He ran across the street.

  They climbed over the fence.

  The car passed through the gate.

Advice or Advise?

- **Advice (noun):** A suggestion or recommendation.
- **Advise (verb):** To give a recommendation.

  Usage:

  "Advice" is a thing: I need your advice on this matter.

  "Advise" is an action: Can you advise me on what to do?

Example Sentences:

My mother always gives good advice.

I would advise you to invest in real estate.

Affect or Effect?

- **Affect (verb):** To influence something.
- **Effect (noun):** The result of an influence.

  Usage:

  "Affect" is an action: The weather can affect your mood.

  "Effect" is the outcome: The effect of the new policy was immediate.

Example Sentences:

The strike affected businesses in Abuja.

The new law had a significant effect on the economy.

Aid or Aide?

- **Aid (noun/verb):** A thing that helps or supports, or the action of helping or providing assistance.

- **Helper (noun):** A person who acts as an assistant or helper, especially in a professional or official capacity.

  Usage:

  "*Aid*" for help or assistance: The charity provided aid to the flood victims.

  "*Aide*" for a person who assists: The politician's aide organised the meeting.

  Example Sentences:

  The new software is designed to aid students in their studies.

  Her aide ensured that all the documents were ready for the meeting.

Aisle or Isle?

- **Aisle (noun):** A passageway between rows of seats, shelves, or other areas, commonly found in churches, theatres, supermarkets, or planes.

- **Isle (noun):** A small island, often used in names of islands.

  Usage:

  "*Aisle*" for a corridor or walkway: She walked down the aisle during the wedding.

  "*Isle*" for an island: They spent their holiday on a peaceful isle.

  Example Sentences:

  Please move your bag to the side of the aisle so others can pass.

  The Isle of Man is a beautiful isle with rich history.

All or Every?

- **All (determiner/pronoun):** Refers to the total number or entirety.

- **Every (determiner):** Refers to each individual member of a group.

  Usage:

  "*All*" refers to the whole: All students must attend the meeting.

  "*Every*" refers to each one: Every student has a different talent.

  Example Sentences:

All Nigerians are proud of their culture.

Every child deserves an education.

All or Whole?

- **All (determiner/pronoun):** Refers to the entirety of a group.
- **Whole (adjective):** Refers to something complete in itself.
  Usage:
    "All" can refer to a collective: All the rice is gone.
    "Whole" refers to something undivided: I ate the whole cake.
  Example Sentences:
    All the money was spent on the project.
    I read the whole book in one day.

Allow, Permit or Let?

- **Allow (verb):** To give permission.
- **Permit (verb):** To formally allow something.
- **Let (verb):** To allow or give permission in a less formal way.
  Usage:
    "Allow" is general: Parents should allow their children to play.
    "Permit" is formal: The company permits employees to work from home.
    "Let" is casual: Please let me go to the party.
  Example Sentences:
    The teacher allowed us to leave early.
    The school permits the use of laptops in class.
    Please let me explain.

Anecdote or Antidote?

- **Anecdote (noun):** A brief, amusing, or interesting story about a real incident or person.
- **Antidote (noun):** A substance that counteracts poison or reduces the harmful effects of something unpleasant.
  Usage:
    "Anecdote" for a short, entertaining story: He shared a funny anecdote about his school days.

"Antidote" for something that neutralises a harmful effect: The doctor quickly administered an antidote for the snakebite.

Example Sentences:

She told an anecdote about her first day at work that made everyone laugh.

The hiker needed an antidote after being bitten by a venomous snake.

Ascent or Assent?

- **Ascent (noun):** The act of climbing or moving upwards, either physically or metaphorically.
- **Assent (noun/verb):** Agreement or approval; to agree or approve.

Usage:

"Ascent" for upward movement: The ascent to the mountain peak was challenging.

"Assent" for agreement: The committee gave their assent to the new proposal.

Example Sentences:

The climbers began their ascent early in the morning to reach the summit by noon.

The manager gave her assent to the new project plan.

Assume or Presume?

- **Assume (verb):** To take something for granted without proof or evidence.
- **Presume (verb):** To believe something is true based on evidence or probability.

Usage:

"Assume" when making a guess without proof: I assume you've already eaten since you're not hungry.

"Presume" when believing something is true based on evidence: Since he has not arrived yet, I presume his flight was delayed.

Example Sentences:

Don't assume everyone knows the rules; make sure to explain them clearly.

The police presume that the suspect acted alone based on the evidence they found.

Assure, Ensure, or Insure?

- **Assure (verb):** To promise or state with confidence, often to provide reassurance.
- **Ensure (verb):** To make certain that something will happen.
- **Insure (verb):** To provide financial protection against loss or damage.
  Usage:

    "Assure" to promise or reassure: I assure you that the project will be completed on time.

    "Ensure" to guarantee or make sure: Please ensure that the door is locked before you leave.

    "Insure" to provide insurance: We need to insure the car before taking it on the road.

  Example Sentences:

    I can assure you that your package will arrive tomorrow.

    Please ensure that all the windows are closed before the storm hits.

    It's wise to insure valuable items like your home or car against potential damage.

All Ready or Already?

- **All Ready (phrase):** Means that everything or everyone is fully prepared or set.
- **Already (adverb):** Refers to something that has happened before now or earlier than expected.

  Usage:

    "All ready" when everyone or everything is prepared: The team is all ready for the match.

    "Already" for something completed earlier: She has already finished her homework.

  Example Sentences:

    We are all ready to leave for the party.

    He already submitted the report yesterday.

Almost or Nearly?

- **Almost (adverb):** Very close to but not exactly.
- **Nearly (adverb):** Almost, but slightly less than.

  Usage:

Both mean the same, but *"almost"* is more common: I almost finished the project.

"Nearly" is used similarly: I nearly missed the bus.

Example Sentences:

The movie is almost over.

We're nearly out of petrol.

Alone, Lonely, or Lonesome?

- **Alone (adjective/adverb):** By oneself.
- **Lonely (adjective):** Feeling sad due to lack of company.
- **Lonesome (adjective):** Similar to "lonely," often used in informal contexts.

Usage:

"Alone" refers to being physically by oneself: I was alone at home.

"Lonely" is an emotional state: She felt lonely after moving to a new city.

"Lonesome" is often used informally, particularly in American English: It's a lonesome road.

Example Sentences:

I live alone in my apartment.

He was lonely after his friend left.

The lonesome house stood at the end of the street.

Along or Alongside?

- **Along (preposition/adverb):** Moving in a line or direction.
- **Alongside (preposition/adverb):** Next to something or someone.
  Usage:

"Along" refers to movement or a line: We walked along the beach.

"Alongside" refers to being beside: The boat sailed alongside the shore.

Example Sentences:

We travelled along the river.

The teacher worked alongside the students.

Already, Still or Yet?

- **Already (adverb):** Before now or earlier than expected.

- **Still (adverb):** Continuation of something.
- **Yet (adverb):** Up to now, often used in questions or negatives.

  Usage:

  "Already" for something done earlier: I've already finished my homework.

  "Still" for something ongoing: I'm still working on it.

  "Yet" for something expected but not done: He hasn't arrived yet.

  Example Sentences:

  I have already eaten dinner.

  Are you still studying?

  Has she replied yet?

Also, As well or Too?

- **Also (adverb):** In addition, typically used at the beginning or middle of a sentence.
- **As well (phrase):** In addition, typically used at the end of a sentence.
- **Too (adverb):** In addition, used at the end of a sentence.

  Usage:

  "Also" adds information: She's a teacher and also a writer.

  "As well" is similar but used at the end: She's a teacher as well.

  "Too" is more common in informal speech: She's a teacher too.

  Example Sentences:

  He works hard, and he also studies.

  She will attend the meeting as well.

  I want to come too.

Alternate(ly), Alternative(ly)

- **Alternate (adjective/verb):** Every other, or to switch between two things.
- **Alternative (adjective/noun):** Another option.

  Usage:

  "Alternate" is for taking turns: We work on alternate days.

  "Alternative" is for different options: We need an alternative plan.

  Example Sentences:

  We attend classes on alternate days.

They offered an alternative solution.

Although or Though?

- **Although (conjunction):** Despite the fact.
- **Though (conjunction/adverb):** Similar to "although," but also used for informal contrast.

  Usage:

  "*Although*" is often used in formal writing: Although it was raining, we went out.

  "*Though*" can be used similarly, but also at the end: It was raining. We went out, though.

  Example Sentences:

  Although the match was tough, we won.

  He's friendly. Though, he can be shy sometimes.

Altogether or All Together?

- **Altogether (adverb):** Completely or in total.
- **All together (phrase):** Everyone or everything in one place.

  Usage:

  "*Altogether*" for totality: It was altogether a good experience.

  "*All together*" when things are grouped: We were all together at the party.

  Example Sentences:

  The project cost N50,000 altogether.

  We went to the event all together.

Amount of, Number of or Quantity of?

- **Amount of (noun):** Used for uncountable nouns.
- **Number of (noun):** Used for countable nouns.
- **Quantity of (noun):** Similar to "amount," but often used in formal contexts.

  Usage:

  "*Amount of*" for things you can't count: The amount of sugar is too much.

  "*Number of*" for things you can count: The number of students is increasing.

"Quantity of" often in formal or technical language: The quantity of goods sold was high.

Example Sentences:

The amount of rainfall was higher this year.

The number of cars on the road is increasing.

The quantity of rice available is sufficient.

Been or Gone?

- **Been (verb):** Past participle of "be," used to indicate that someone has visited a place and returned.

- **Gone (verb):** Past participle of "go," used to indicate that someone has left and is still away.

   Usage:

   "Been" is used when someone has visited and come back: *I've been to Abuja (and I'm back now).*

   "Gone" is used when someone has left and is still away: *He's gone to Abuja (and hasn't returned).*

   Example Sentences:

   I've been to Lagos several times.

   She's gone to the market.

Begin or Start?

- **Begin (verb):** To commence or initiate something.

- **Start (verb):** To cause something to happen or come into existence.

   Usage:

   "Begin" is often used in formal contexts: *The meeting will begin at 10 am.*

   "Start" is more informal and common in everyday speech: *Let's start the game.*

   Example Sentences:

   The ceremony will begin shortly.

   They started the project last week.

Beside or Besides?

- **Beside (preposition):** Next to or at the side of.

- **Besides (preposition/adverb):** In addition to or apart from.

   Usage:

"Beside" is used for physical proximity: *She sat beside her brother.*

"Besides" is used to add information or to mean "apart from": *Besides football, he likes basketball.*

Example Sentences:

The chair is beside the bed.

Besides cooking, I enjoy reading.

Between or Among?

- **Between (preposition):** Refers to two or more distinct items or individuals.

- **Among (preposition):** Refers to being in the midst of a group or things that are not distinct.

  Usage:

  "Between" is used for distinct items: *The secret is between you and me.*

  "Among" is used when referring to a group: *She was popular among her peers.*

  Example Sentences:

  Choose between these two dresses.

  He's well-respected among his colleagues.

Born or Borne?

- **Born (verb):** The past participle of "bear" (when related to birth).

- **Borne (verb):** The past participle of "bear," meaning carried or endured.

  Usage:

  "Born" refers to birth: *She was born in Lagos.*

  "Borne" refers to something carried or endured: *The costs were borne by the company.*

  Example Sentences:

  I was born in Nigeria.

  The burden was borne by the community.

Bring, Take, and Fetch

- **Bring (verb):** To carry something towards the speaker.

- **Take (verb):** To carry something away from the speaker.

- **Fetch (verb):** To go get something and return with it.

  Usage:

"Bring" when something is coming to you: *Please bring your book to class.*

"Take" when something is going away from you: *Take this letter to your teacher.*

"Fetch" when retrieving something: *Can you fetch the ball for me?*

Example Sentences:

Bring the documents to my office.

Take this food to Mama.

Please fetch me some water.

Can, Could or May?

- **Can** (verb): Indicates ability or possibility.
- **Could** (verb): The past form of "can," used for polite requests or hypothetical situations.
- **May** (verb): Indicates permission or possibility, often more formal.
Usage:

"Can" for ability: *I can swim.*

"Could" for polite requests: *Could you help me with this?*

"May" for formal permission: *May I come in?*

Example Sentences:

Can you solve this problem?

Could you please pass the salt?

May I leave the room?

Childish or Childlike?

- **Childish** (adjective): Describes behaviour that is immature, unreasonable, or bratty, often in a negative way.
- **Childlike** (adjective): Describes qualities that are positive and reminiscent of a child, such as innocence, sweetness, or purity.
Usage:

"Childish" for negative, immature behaviour: *His childish outburst embarrassed everyone.*

"Childlike" for positive, innocent qualities: *She has a childlike sense of wonder.*

Example Sentences:

Throwing a tantrum like that is very childish.

Her childlike enthusiasm for the festival was contagious.

Complement or Compliment?

- **Complement** (noun/verb): Refers to something that completes, enhances, or perfects another thing.
- **Compliment** (noun/verb): Refers to a polite expression of praise or admiration.
  Usage:

    "Complement" for something that completes: *The wine was a perfect complement to the meal.*

    "Compliment" for praise or flattery: *He gave her a compliment on her new dress.*

Example Sentences:

    The scarf really complements your outfit.

    She smiled when he complimented her on her presentation.

Comprise

- **Comprise** (verb): Means to contain, consist of, or be composed of; the whole comprises its parts.

Usage:

    Use "comprise" correctly to mean the whole containing its parts: *The library comprises thousands of books.*

    Avoid the incorrect use of "comprised of": *The committee comprises five members* (not *comprised of five members*).

Example Sentences:

    The country comprises 36 states and the Federal Capital Territory.

    The meal comprises three courses: starter, main, and dessert.

Classic or Classical?

- **Classic** (adjective/noun): Something that is a perfect example of its kind or has lasting significance.

- **Classical** (adjective): Related to ancient Greek or Roman culture, or traditional forms of music or art.

Usage:

    "Classic" describes something iconic or timeless: *That car is a classic.*

    "Classical" refers to ancient culture or traditional forms: *He loves classical music.*

Example Sentences:

That novel is a classic of Nigerian literature.

She enjoys listening to classical music.

Come or Go?

- **Come** (verb): To move towards the speaker.
- **Go** (verb): To move away from the speaker.

Usage:

"Come" is used when the movement is towards you: *Please come here.*

"Go" is used when the movement is away from you: *Go to your room.*

Example Sentences:

Come to my house tomorrow.

Go and meet your friend.

Consider or Regard?

- **Consider** (verb): To think about something carefully before making a decision.
- **Regard** (verb): To think of something in a particular way or hold in esteem.

Usage:

"Consider" for thoughtful evaluation: *Consider your options before deciding.*

"Regard" for holding an opinion: *She is highly regarded in her field.*

Example Sentences:

I will consider your proposal.

He is regarded as the best player on the team.

Consist, Comprise or Compose?

- **Consist** (verb): To be made up of.
- **Comprise** (verb): To include or contain; often used incorrectly to mean "consist of."
- **Compose** (verb): To make up or form the substance of something.

Usage:

"Consist" for what something is made of: *The team consists of five players.*

"Comprise" for what is included: *The committee comprises five members.*

"Compose" for what forms something: *The committee is composed of five members.*

Example Sentences:

The dish consists of rice and beans.

The council comprises 10 elected officials.

The board is composed of experts in various fields.

Content or Contents?

- **Content** (noun): The subject or topics covered in a book, document, or conversation.
- **Contents** (noun): The things contained in something, like a box or bag.

Usage:

"Content" refers to information: *The content of the lecture was fascinating.*

"Contents" refers to physical items: *The contents of the bag were scattered.*

Example Sentences:

The content of the article was informative.

She emptied the contents of her purse on the table.

Continual or Continuous?

- **Continual** (adjective): Refers to something that happens repeatedly with interruptions.
- **Continuous** (adjective): Refers to something that happens without stopping, without any breaks or pauses.

Usage:

"Continual" for repeated actions with pauses: *The continual ringing of the phone was annoying.*

"Continuous" for something that goes on without interruption: *The machine operates in continuous motion.*

Example Sentences:

The generator had continual issues, breaking down every few days.

The continuous hum of the air conditioner made it hard to concentrate.

Convince or Persuade?

- **Convince** (verb): Means to make someone believe or accept something as true, usually through reasoning or evidence.

- **Persuade** (verb): Means to cause someone to do something through reasoning, argument, or other forms of influence, including emotion or pressure.

Usage:

"Convince" for changing someone's belief or perspective: *The evidence convinced her that the project was worth the investment.*

"Persuade" for influencing someone to take action: *He persuaded his friend to join the team.*

Example Sentences:

After seeing the results, I was convinced that the new strategy would work.

She persuaded him to attend the meeting, but he wasn't fully convinced it was necessary.

e.g. or i.e.?

These two abbreviations are often mistakenly used as if they mean the same thing, but they serve different purposes.
i.e. means "in other words" or "that is," while **e.g.** means "for example."

Example Sentences:

- *Comedians like Richard Pryor and George Carlin (i.e., pioneers of modern stand-up comedy) changed the landscape of humour in the 1970s.*

- *The pioneers of modern stand-up comedy (e.g., Richard Pryor and George Carlin) changed the landscape of humour in the 1970s.*

Eke Out

This phrase is often understood as "barely managing to survive."

Original meanings:

- "To supplement": *I eke out my income by taking on additional projects.*

- "To stretch out": *We eked out the last of our resources to make them last until payday.*

Example Sentences:

- I eke out a living as a freelancer.

- We eked out the last of the supplies until reinforcements arrived.

Elder, Eldest or Older, Oldest?

- **Elder/Eldest** (adjective/noun): Used when comparing the age of people, often in a family context.

- **Older/Oldest** (adjective): More general, can be used for people and things.

Usage:

"Elder/Eldest" for family relationships: *He is my elder brother.*

"Older/Oldest" for general use: *She is older than her classmates.*

Example Sentences:

My elder sister is a doctor.

The oldest tree in the village is over 100 years old.

Emigrate or Immigrate?

- **Emigrate** (verb): To leave one's country or region with the intention of settling in another. Always used with the preposition "from."
- **Immigrate** (verb): To come to live permanently in a foreign country. Always used with the preposition "to."

Example Sentences:

He emigrated from Ghana to the UK in search of better opportunities.

She immigrated to the United States from Nigeria.

Remember: You emigrate *from* a place and immigrate *to* a place.

Eminent or Imminent?

- **Eminent** (adjective): Describes someone or something that is highly respected, famous, or distinguished in a particular field.
- **Imminent** (adjective): Describes something that is about to happen very soon, often with a sense of urgency.

Example Sentences:

- Dr. Adichie is an eminent scholar in African literature.
- The arrival of the storm is imminent, so we should take cover immediately.

Remember: An eminent person is famous, while an imminent event is about to happen.

Empathy or Sympathy?

- **Empathy** (noun): Involves understanding and sharing the feelings of another person.
- **Sympathy** (noun): Involves feeling compassion, sorrow, or pity for the hardships that another person encounters.

Example Sentences:

Her empathy for the victims of the flood led her to organize a relief effort.

He sent a card to express his sympathy for the loss of her father.

Remember: Empathy is about sharing feelings; sympathy is about recognizing and caring about someone's suffering.

Emulate or Imitate?

- **Emulate** (verb): To strive to equal or excel someone, often by imitating them, with the goal of surpassing or matching their achievements.
- **Imitate** (verb): To copy someone's actions, behaviour, or style, without necessarily aiming to surpass the original.

Example Sentences:

She always tried to emulate her older brother's academic success.

Children often imitate their parents' mannerisms.

Remember: Emulate has an aspirational connotation, while imitate is more about straightforward copying.

Epitome

- **Epitome** (noun): Refers to a person or thing that is the perfect example of a particular quality or type.

Example Sentence:

She is the epitome of kindness, always going out of her way to help others.

Usage Tip: The epitome is not necessarily the best, but it is the perfect example of something.

etc. or et al.?

- **etc.** (abbreviation for "et cetera"): Used at the end of a list to indicate that there are other items not listed. It means "and the rest" or "and so on."

- **et al.** (abbreviation for "et alia"): Used in academic or formal writing to indicate that additional people are involved in something but are not named. It means "and others."

Example Sentences:

Please bring your textbooks, notebooks, pens, etc. to class.

The research was conducted by Dr. Okafor, Dr. Ali, et al.

Remember: Use "etc." for things and "et al." for people.

End or Finish?

- **End** (noun/verb): The final point or part of something.

- **Finish** (verb): To bring something to completion.

Usage:

"End" refers to the conclusion: *The movie ended at 9 pm.*

"Finish" refers to completing something: *I finished my homework early.*

Example Sentences:

The match will end soon.

Please finish your meal.

Especially or Specially?

- **Especially** (adverb): Used to single out something as more important or true.
- **Specially** (adverb): Indicates something done for a particular purpose.

Usage:

"Especially" for emphasis: *I love fruits, especially mangoes.*

"Specially" for a specific purpose: *This cake was specially made for you.*

Example Sentences:

She is especially talented in music.

The clothes were specially tailored for the event.

Except or Except for?

- **Except** (preposition/conjunction): Excluding something from a statement.
- **Except for** (preposition): Used to introduce an exception to a general statement.

Usage:

"Except" for exclusion: *Everyone passed except John.*

"Except for" is used in the same way but adds emphasis on what is being excluded: *The trip was fine except for the traffic.*

Example Sentences:

Everyone came to the party except Tunde.

The day was perfect except for the rain.

Impact or Affect?

- **Impact (verb):** Although commonly used as a synonym for "affect," this usage is often incorrect. "Impact" originally means "to pack tightly

together," as in an impacted tooth. It's better to use "affect" when describing how something influences or changes another thing.

Example:

The new policy will affect property taxes.

Usage Tip: Use "affect" when you want to describe an influence or change, not "impact."

- **Impact (noun)**: As a noun, "impact" refers to the force or effect of one thing striking another.

  Example:

  The impact of the collision damaged the car.

In or At?

- **In (preposition)**: Used to indicate location or position within a larger area or space.
- **At (preposition)**: Used to indicate a specific point or place.

Usage:

"In" for general locations: She is in the office.

"At" for specific points: He is at the entrance.

Example Sentences:

I live in Lagos.

Let's meet at the café.

Injure, Wound or Hurt?

- **Injure (verb)**: To cause physical harm, often used for accidents.
- **Wound (verb/noun)**: To cause injury, typically in a violent manner, or the injury itself.
- **Hurt (verb)**: To cause pain or damage, both physical and emotional.

Usage:

"Injure" for accidents: He injured his leg in a fall.

"Wound" for violence: The soldier was wounded in battle.

"Hurt" for general pain: My head hurts.

Example Sentences:

She injured her back while lifting.

The cut left a deep wound.

The comment hurt his feelings.

Intelligent, Smart or Clever?

- **Intelligent (adjective):** Having or showing high mental capability.
- **Smart (adjective):** Quick-witted or bright; can also mean well-dressed.
- **Clever (adjective):** Mentally sharp, inventive, or resourceful.

Usage:

"Intelligent" for overall mental ability: She is an intelligent student.

"Smart" for quick thinking or fashion: He gave a smart answer.

"Clever" for inventiveness: That's a clever solution.

Example Sentences:

The scientist is highly intelligent.

You look smart in that suit.

She made a clever remark.

Journey, Trip, Travel or Tour?

- **Journey (noun):** The act of travelling from one place to another, especially long distances.
- **Trip (noun):** A short journey or an excursion.
- **Travel (noun/verb):** The act of moving from place to place.
- **Tour (noun):** A journey for pleasure where several places are visited.

Usage:

"Journey" for long-distance travel: The journey to Abuja was tiring.

"Trip" for short visits: We took a trip to the countryside.

"Travel" for the general concept: She loves to travel.

"Tour" for sightseeing: The tour covered five cities.

Example Sentences:

The journey took three days.

Our trip to the beach was fun.

He travels frequently for work.

They went on a European tour.

Join, Attend or Participate?

- **Join (verb):** To become a member of a group or take part in an activity.
- **Attend (verb):** To be present at an event.
- **Participate (verb):** To take an active part in an event or activity.

Usage:

"Join" for becoming part of something: I joined the book club.

"Attend" for being present: She attended the conference.

"Participate" for actively taking part: He participated in the discussion.

Example Sentences:

I plan to join the meeting.

Will you attend the seminar?

Many people participated in the rally.

Kind, Sort or Type?

- **Kind (noun):** A group of people or things having similar characteristics.
- **Sort (noun):** A particular kind or variety.
- **Type (noun):** A category of people or things sharing similar characteristics.

Usage:

"Kind" for general categories: This kind of book is very popular.

"Sort" for informal grouping: He's not the sort of person who lies.

"Type" for classification: What type of food do you like?

Example Sentences:

They sell all kinds of fruits.

She's a different sort of manager.

My favourite type of music is jazz.

Know or Meet?

- **Know (verb):** To be aware of or familiar with someone or something.
- **Meet (verb):** To encounter or come into contact with someone for the first time.

Usage:

"Know" for familiarity: I know her from school.

"Meet" for initial encounters: We met at the conference.

Example Sentences:

Do you know the new manager?

I met him yesterday.

Expect, Hope or Wait?

- **Expect** (verb): To think something will happen.
- **Hope** (verb): To want something to happen.
- **Wait** (verb): To stay until something happens.

Usage:

> "Expect" when you think something will happen: *I expect the results tomorrow.*
>
> "Hope" when you wish for something: *I hope it doesn't rain.*
>
> "Wait" when you stay until something happens: *I'll wait for you at the bus stop.*

Example Sentences:

> *We expect a delivery today.*
>
> *I hope you can come.*
>
> *Wait here until I return.*

Experience or Experiment?

- **Experience** (noun/verb): Practical contact with and observation of facts or events.
- **Experiment** (noun/verb): A scientific procedure to test a hypothesis.

Usage:

> "Experience" for what you've been through: *She has a lot of experience in teaching.*
>
> "Experiment" for testing ideas: *The students conducted an experiment in chemistry.*

Example Sentences:

> *He has years of experience in banking.*
>
> *We experimented with different recipes.*

Fall or Fall Down?

- **Fall** (verb): To drop from a higher position.
- **Fall down** (phrasal verb): To drop suddenly to the ground.

Usage:

> "Fall" is general: *Leaves fall from the trees.*
>
> "Fall down" is specific to dropping to the ground: *He tripped and fell down.*

Example Sentences:

> *The prices will fall soon.*
>
> *I watched the vase fall down.*

Far or A Long Way?

- **Far** (adjective/adverb): At a great distance.
- **A long way** (phrase): A great distance.

Usage:

"Far" is shorter and more common: *How far is your house?*
"A long way" adds emphasis: *The village is a long way from here.*

Example Sentences:

Abuja is far from here.
We walked a long way to get here.

Farther, Farthest or Further, Furthest?

- **Farther/Farthest** (adjective/adverb): Used for physical distances.
- **Further/Furthest** (adjective/adverb): Used for metaphorical or physical distances.

Usage:

"Farther/Farthest" for literal distance: *The market is farther than I thought.*

"Further/Furthest" for both literal and metaphorical: *We need to discuss this further.*

Example Sentences:

The school is farther from my house.

He has gone further in his career than anyone else.

Fast, Quick or Quickly?

- **Fast** (adjective/adverb): Moving or capable of moving at high speed.
- **Quick** (adjective): Done with speed or rapidly.
- **Quickly** (adverb): In a quick manner.

Usage:

"Fast" for high speed: *He drives a fast car.*

"Quick" for promptness: *He gave a quick response.*

"Quickly" for the manner of doing something: *She finished her homework quickly.*

Example Sentences:

The internet here is very fast.

I need a quick answer.

She ran quickly to catch the bus.

Fell or Felt?

- **Fell** (verb): The past tense of "fall."
- **Felt** (verb): The past tense of "feel."

Usage:

> "Fell" when something drops: *He fell off his bike.*
>
> "Felt" when referring to emotions or sensations: *I felt happy yesterday.*

Example Sentences:

> *I fell asleep during the movie.*
>
> *He felt cold in the morning.*

Fewer or Less?

- **Fewer** (adjective): Use "fewer" when referring to things that can be counted individually. It is used with countable nouns (things you can number, like "reasons," "apples," or "books").

Example: *I now have fewer reasons to attend the event.*

Usage Tip: If you can count the items, use "fewer."

- **Less** (adjective): Use "less" when referring to things that cannot be counted individually. It is used with uncountable nouns (things that are measured, like "money," "time," or "water").

Example: *We have less time to finish the project.*

Usage Tip: If you cannot count the items, and they are measured as a whole, use "less."

Exception:

When referring to specific measurements of money, distance, time, or weight, "less" is used even though these can be counted. This is because these are seen as singular quantities rather than individual units.

Example: *The trip cost less than fifty thousand naira.*

Explanation: Here, "fifty thousand naira" is treated as a lump sum rather than individual naira notes.

Summary:

Use "fewer" for things you can count individually: fewer apples, fewer reasons, fewer cars.

Use "less" for things that are measured as a whole: less time, less water, less money.

Exception:

For specific measurements of money, distance, time, or weight, use "less," not "fewer": less than ten kilometres, less than a million naira, less than two hours.

Female or Feminine; Male or Masculine?

- **Female/Male (noun/adjective):** Biological sex.
- **Feminine/Masculine (adjective):** Traits typically associated with females/males.

Usage:

"Female/Male" for sex: *There are more female students in the class.*

"Feminine/Masculine" for qualities: *She has a feminine style.*

Example Sentences:

The team has both **male** and **female** members.

His voice is very **masculine**.

Finally, At Last, Lastly or In the End?

- **Finally (adverb):** After a long time.
- **At last (phrase):** After a long wait or delay.
- **Lastly (adverb):** Used to introduce the last item.
- **In the end (phrase):** The final result or conclusion.

Usage:

"Finally" and "At last" are similar: *Finally, we arrived at the hotel.*

"Lastly" for concluding: *Lastly, I want to thank you all.*

"In the end" for outcome: *In the end, everything was fine.*

Example Sentences:

Finally, he agreed to help.

At last, the rain stopped.

Lastly, don't forget your homework.

In the end, they decided not to go.

First, Firstly or At First?

- **First (adjective/adverb):** Coming before all others.
- **Firstly (adverb):** Used to introduce the first point in a list.
- **At first (phrase):** Refers to the beginning of something.

Usage:

"First" and "Firstly" to indicate order: *First, I need to make a call.*

"At first" for initial impressions: *At first, I didn't like the idea.*

Example Sentences:

First, we need to talk.

Firstly, let me explain the rules.

At first, I was nervous.

Fit or Suit?

- **Fit (verb/adjective):** To be the right size or shape.
- **Suit (verb):** To be appropriate or acceptable.

Usage:

"Fit" for physical size: *This dress fits you perfectly.*

"Suit" for being appropriate: *This job suits him well.*

Example Sentences:

The shoes don't **fit**.

That colour **suits** you.

Following or The Following?

- **Following (preposition/adjective):** Coming after something else.
- **The Following (adjective):** Refers to what comes next in a sequence.

Usage:

"Following" for after something: *Following the meeting, we had lunch.*

"The following" to introduce a list: *Please read the following instructions.*

Example Sentences:

Following the announcement, there was silence.

The following people have passed the exam.

For or Since?

- **For (preposition):** Refers to the duration of time.
- **Since (preposition/conjunction):** Refers to the starting point of an action that continues.

Usage:

"For" indicates how long: *I've lived here for five years.*

"Since" indicates when something started: *I've lived here since 2015.*

Example Sentences:

I've been waiting **for** two hours.

He has been working here **since** January.

Forget or Leave?

- **Forget (verb):** To fail to remember.
- **Leave (verb):** To go away from something or to allow something to remain.

Usage:

> "Forget" for memory lapses: *Don't forget your keys.*
>
> "Leave" for departing or letting something stay: *I left my bag at home.*

Example Sentences:

> Please don't **forget** my birthday.
>
> He **left** his book on the table.

Full or Filled?

- **Full (adjective):** Holding as much as possible.
- **Filled (adjective/verb):** Having something put into it until it's full.

Usage:

> "Full" indicates no more space: *The bottle is full of water.*
>
> "Filled" indicates that something was added: *The bottle is filled with water.*

Example Sentences:

> My cup is **full**.
>
> The tank was **filled** with petrol.

Fun or Funny?

- **Fun (noun/adjective):** Enjoyable or amusing.
- **Funny (adjective):** Causing laughter.

Usage:

> "Fun" for enjoyment: *The party was fun.*
>
> "Funny" for humour: *That joke was funny.*

Example Sentences:

> We had a lot of **fun** at the beach.
>
> The comedian was really **funny**.

Get or Go?

- **Get (verb):** To obtain or receive something.
- **Go (verb):** To move or travel to a place.

Usage:

> "Get" for receiving: *I got a new phone.*
>
> "Go" for moving: *I'm going to the market.*

Example Sentences:

> Did you **get** my message?
>
> Let's **go** to the park.

Grateful or Thankful?

- **Grateful (adjective):** Feeling or showing appreciation.
- **Thankful (adjective):** Feeling or expressing gratitude, especially for something that has happened.

Usage:

> "Grateful" for deep appreciation: *I am grateful for your help.*
>
> "Thankful" for relief or happiness: *I'm thankful that the exam is over.*

Example Sentences:

> I am **grateful** for your support.
>
> We are **thankful** that the rain stopped.

Hear or Listen (to)?

- **Hear (verb):** To perceive sound.
- **Listen (to) (verb):** To actively pay attention to sound.

Usage:

> "Hear" for the act of perceiving sound: *I can hear music.*
>
> "Listen to" for actively focusing on sound: *Please listen to the instructions.*

Example Sentences:

> I can **hear** the rain outside.
>
> **Listen to** the teacher carefully.

High or Tall?

- **High (adjective):** Describes something that is at a significant height or distance above the ground.
- **Tall (adjective):** Describes something with considerable height, often in relation to a person or structure.

Usage:

"High" for elevation or distance above the ground: *The mountain is very high.*

"Tall" for describing height: *She is very tall.*

Example Sentences:

The wall is **high** and difficult to climb.

The giraffe is **tall**.

Historic or Historical?

- **Historic (adjective):** Something famous or important in history.
- **Historical (adjective):** Related to or concerning history or past events.

Usage:

"Historic" for something significant: *The signing of the agreement was a historic event.*

"Historical" for things related to history: *He studies historical documents.*

Example Sentences:

The visit to the museum was **historic**.

The movie is based on **historical** events.

House or Home?

- **House (noun):** A building where people live.
- **Home (noun):** A place where one lives, often with emotional or personal significance.

Usage:

"House" for the physical structure: *The house is on Main Street.*

"Home" for where one feels a sense of belonging: *Home is where the heart is.*

Example Sentences:

We just bought a new **house**.

Lagos will always be my **home**.

How is …? or What is … like?

- **How is …? (question phrase):** Asks about the condition, state, or feelings of something or someone.
- **What is … like? (question phrase):** Asks for a description or explanation of something or someone.

Usage:

"How is ...?" for the current state: *How is your project going?*

"What is ... like?" for description: *What is the weather like?*

Example Sentences:

How is your brother feeling now?

What is your new job **like**?

If or When?

- **If (conjunction):** Used to introduce a conditional clause.

- **When (conjunction):** Used to refer to a time or event.

Usage:

"If" for conditions: *If it rains, we will cancel the picnic.*

"When" for certain events: *When he arrives, we will start the meeting.*

Example Sentences:

If you need help, call me.

When I finish work, I'll go home.

If or Whether?

- **If (conjunction):** Used to introduce a conditional clause.

- **Whether (conjunction):** Used when expressing doubt between two alternatives.

Usage:

"If" for conditions: *If it rains, take an umbrella.*

"Whether" for uncertainty: *She is unsure whether to go or stay.*

Example Sentences:

If you see him, tell him to call me.

I don't know **whether** she will attend the event.

Ill or Sick?

- **Ill (adjective):** Unwell or suffering from a disease (more formal).

- **Sick (adjective):** Unwell or feeling nauseous (more common in informal contexts).

Usage:

"Ill" for a formal expression of unwellness: *He has been ill for a week.*

"Sick" for more casual contexts: *She is feeling sick today.*

Example Sentences:

He was absent because he was **ill**.

I feel **sick** after eating too much.

Impact vs. Affect

- **Impact (verb):** Although commonly used as a synonym for "affect," this usage is often incorrect. "Impact" originally means "to pack tightly together," as in an impacted tooth. It's better to use "affect" when describing how something influences or changes another thing.

  Example: *The new policy will **affect** property taxes.*

  > **Usage Tip:** Use "affect" when you want to describe an influence or change, not "impact."

- **Impact (noun):** As a noun, "impact" refers to the force or effect of one thing striking another.

  Example: *The impact of the collision damaged the car.*

Imply vs. Infer

- **Imply (verb):** The speaker or writer "implies" when they suggest something indirectly.

  Example: *She **implied** that I was late by mentioning the time.*

  Usage Tip: "Imply" is what you do when you hint at something without saying it directly.

- **Infer (verb):** The listener or reader "infers" when they deduce or conclude something from what is implied.

  Example: *I **inferred** that she was upset because she didn't smile.*

  Usage Tip: "Infer" is what you do when you pick up on a hint or conclude something based on indirect information.

In Order To vs. To

- **In Order To (phrase):** Sometimes necessary, but often an unnecessarily formal way to say "to."

  Example: *We should exercise **to** stay healthy.*

  Usage Tip: Drop "in order" when "to" works just fine.

In Regard(s) To, With Regard(s) To

- **In Regard To / With Regard To (phrases):** These phrases mean "concerning" or "about." They should not be pluralized.

  Example: *With **regard to** your request, I'll get back to you tomorrow.*

  Usage Tip: Use "regard" without an "s" when using these phrases.

- **As Regards (phrase):** Means the same as "in regard to" or "with regard to" but is often pluralized incorrectly.

  Example: *As **regards** your request, I'll get back to you tomorrow.*

  Usage Tip: "As regards" is correct with the "s."

Regardless

- **Irregardless (nonstandard):** This word is a mistake resulting from the confusion between "regardless" and "irrespective." It should not be used.
  Correct Term: *Regardless*

  Explanation: "Irregardless" is technically a double negative and should be avoided.

Imply or Infer?

- **Imply (verb):** To suggest something indirectly.

- **Infer (verb):** To deduce or conclude information from evidence.

Usage:

> "Imply" for suggesting: *His tone implied that he was unhappy.*

> "Infer" for deducing: *From his tone, I inferred he was unhappy.*

Example Sentences:

> The article **implies** that changes are needed.

> From her reaction, I **inferred** she was surprised.

In the Way or On the Way?

- **In the Way (phrase):** Obstructing or blocking a path.

- **On the Way (phrase):** Progressing towards a destination or goal.

Usage:

> "In the way" for obstruction: *The chair is in the way.*

> "On the way" for progress: *I'm on the way to work.*

Example Sentences:

> The car parked **in the way** of the entrance.

> He is **on the way** to success.

It's or Its?

- **It's (contraction):** It is or it has.

- **Its (pronoun):** Belonging to it.

Usage:

"It's" for contractions: *It's raining outside.*

"Its" for possession: *The dog wagged its tail.*

Example Sentences:

It's going to be a long day.

The company is known for **its** innovation.

Lay, Lie

"Lay" and "lie" are often confusing because they sound similar but have different meanings and uses. Understanding how to use them correctly is essential.

Lie (to recline):

- **Present:** *I **lie** on the bed to rest.*

- **Present Continuous:** *I am **lying** on the bed now.*

- **Past:** *I **lay** on the bed yesterday.*

- **Present Perfect:** *I have **other** on the bed many times.*

Lay (to put or place something):

- **Present:** *Please **lay** the book on the table.*

- **Present Continuous:** *I am **laying** the book on the table.*

- **Past:** *I **laid** the book on the table yesterday.*

- **Present Perfect:** *I have **laid** the book on the table several times.*

Examples:

Incorrect: *I'm going to lay on the couch.* **Correct:** *I'm going to lie on the couch.*

Incorrect: *Your wallet is laying on the dresser.* **Correct:** *Your wallet is lying on the dresser.*

Incorrect: *He wants to lay down.* **Correct:** *He wants to lie down.*

Yesterday I *(guessed as "laid" but correct is "lay")* **on the bed. Correct:** *Yesterday I lay on the bed.*

I have often *(guessed as "laid" but correct is "lain")* **on the bed. Correct:** *I have often lain on the bed.*

I have often *(guessed as "laid" but correct is "laid")* **my wallet on the dresser. Correct:** *I have often laid my wallet on the dresser.*

Using "lie" means reclining or resting, while "lay" refers to placing something down. Keep these distinctions in mind to avoid confusion.

Example Sentences:

Lay the blanket on the bed.

I need to **lie** down for a while.

Present Tense:

- **Recline:** *I enjoy to **lie** on the sofa to relax after work.*
- **Recline (continuous):** *I am **lying** on the sofa right now.*
- **Put/Place:** *Please **lay** the box on the shelf.*
- **Put/Place (continuous):** *I am **laying** the box on the shelf.*
- **Tell a Falsehood:** *I am tempted to **lie** about my plans.*
- **Tell a Falsehood (continuous):** *I am not **lying** about my plans.*

Past Tense:

- **Recline:** *I **lay** on the sofa for a few hours yesterday.*
- **Put/Place:** *I **laid** the box on the shelf earlier today.*
- **Tell a Falsehood:** *He **lied** during the interview.*

Past Tense with a Helping Verb (has, have):

- **Recline:** *I have **other** on the sofa every weekend this month.*
- **Put/Place:** *I have **laid** the box on the shelf where it belongs.*
- **Tell a Falsehood:** *He has **lied** multiple times about his whereabouts.*

These examples use different contexts and actions while demonstrating the correct usage of "lay," "lie," and "lie" (as in telling a falsehood) in various tenses.

Lend or Borrow?

- **Lend (verb):** To give something to someone temporarily.
- **Borrow (verb):** To take something from someone temporarily.

Usage:

"Lend" for giving: *I will lend you my pen.*

"Borrow" for taking: *Can I borrow your pen?*

Example Sentences:

She agreed to **lend** me her car.

I need to **borrow** some money.

Less or Fewer?

- **Less (adjective):** Used with uncountable nouns.
- **Fewer (adjective):** Used with countable nouns.

Usage:

"Less" for uncountable quantities: *I have less time today.*

"Fewer" for countable items: *Fewer students attended the class.*

Example Sentences:

I need **less** sugar in my tea.

There are **fewer** people at the event this year.

Let Him Who Is Guiltless...

A commonly misquoted phrase is "Let he who is without sin cast the first stone." This error has confused people for years. The correct wording from the Bible, specifically the Gospel of John, is "He that is without sin among you, let him first cast a stone at her."

Explanation: The confusion arises from using "he" instead of "him." In English grammar, "him" is the correct form because it is the object of the verb "let." When you say, "Let him cast the first stone," "him" is receiving the action, so it must be in the objective case.

Incorrect: Let he who is without sin cast the first stone.

Correct: Let him who is without sin cast the first stone.

Summary: "Him" should be used instead of "he" because it correctly functions as the object of the verb.

Like

People often use "like" in ways that can cause confusion, especially in formal writing or speech. For instance, saying, "Do it like she does," may sound right in conversation, but grammatically, it's not ideal.

Explanation: Like is primarily a preposition, meaning "similar to." It should be used to compare nouns or pronouns without a verb following immediately. If a verb follows, such as in "like she does," the correct word to use is "as" or "the way."

Incorrect: Do it like she does.

Correct: Do it the way she does.

Correct: Say it as if you mean it.

Summary: Use "like" to compare things without a verb following. If there's a verb after, switch to "as" or "the way."

Literally

The word "literally" is often used incorrectly to emphasise something that isn't literally true. For example, someone might say, "I was so scared, I literally jumped out of my skin." Unless they've experienced something supernatural, this is an incorrect use of "literally."

Explanation: Literally means something happened exactly as described, with no exaggeration or metaphor. When you say, "I literally couldn't

believe my eyes," you mean that you were physically unable to see it or process it. To avoid misusing "literally," consider using alternatives like "virtually" or "practically" for dramatic effect without distorting the truth.

Incorrect: I was so tired, I literally died of exhaustion.

Correct: I was so tired, I virtually collapsed from exhaustion.

Summary: Use "literally" only for factual statements. For exaggeration, opt for "virtually" or "practically."

Loose vs. Lose

These two words are often confused, but they have distinct meanings and uses.

- **Loose** (Adjective): Means something is not tight or securely fastened.
- **Lose** (Verb): Means to misplace something or to fail to win.

Examples:

> **Loose**: My shoe is loose, and I need to tie it properly.

> **Lose**: If I'm not careful, I might lose my phone.

Summary: Remember, "loose" describes something that isn't tight, while "lose" refers to misplacing something or not winning.

Media

The term **media** is often misused as a singular noun, but it is actually a plural noun. The singular form is **medium**, which refers to one form of communication, such as television, radio, or newspapers.

Explanation: Since "media" is plural, it should be paired with plural verbs like "are" or "have." For instance, it's incorrect to say, "The media is biassed." Instead, say, "The media are biassed." This recognises that "media" includes multiple platforms or sources.

Incorrect: The media is spreading misinformation.

Correct: The media are spreading misinformation.

Summary: Always treat "media" as a plural noun and pair it with plural verbs to acknowledge its diverse nature.

Look at, See or Watch?

- **Look at (verb):** To direct your eyes towards something intentionally.
- **See (verb):** To perceive with the eyes without necessarily focusing.
- **Watch (verb):** To observe something attentively, usually for a period of time.

Usage:

"Look at" for intentional focus: *Look at the painting.*

"See" for general perception: *Did you see the rainbow?*

"Watch" for focused observation: *Watch the movie carefully.*

Example Sentences:

Look at the stars in the sky.

Did you **see** that car?

Let's **watch** a film tonight.

Low or Short?

- **Low (adjective):** Not high or tall; a small distance from the ground.
- **Short (adjective):** Having less length or height.

Usage:

"Low" for something not high: *The ceiling is low in this room.*

"Short" for describing lesser height or length: *He is shorter than his brother.*

Example Sentences:

The chair is too **low** for the table.

She has **short** hair.

Man, Mankind or People?

- **Man (noun):** Refers to an adult male human being.
- **Mankind (noun):** Refers to all human beings collectively.
- **People (noun):** Refers to human beings collectively, used more commonly and inclusively than "mankind."

Usage:

"Man" for an individual male: *The man is very tall.*

"Mankind" for all human beings: *Mankind has explored space.*

"People" for human beings collectively: *People are enjoying the festival.*

Example Sentences:

The **man** spoke at the conference.

Mankind has made great technological advances.

The **people** in the village are very friendly.

Maybe or May Be?

- **Maybe (adverb):** Possibly or perhaps.

- **May be (verb phrase):** Expresses possibility, with "may" as a modal verb and "be" as a verb.

Usage:

"Maybe" to express possibility: *Maybe it will rain tomorrow.*

"May be" as part of a verb phrase: *She may be at the party tonight.*

Example Sentences:

Maybe we should go out for dinner.

He **may be** the person you're looking for.

Maybe or Perhaps?

- **Maybe (adverb):** Used informally to indicate a possibility.
- **Perhaps (adverb):** A more formal way to indicate a possibility.

Usage:

"Maybe" in informal contexts: *Maybe I'll join you later.*

"Perhaps" in more formal or written contexts: *Perhaps we should consider another option.*

Example Sentences:

Maybe you're right.

Perhaps you could explain that again.

Nearest or Next?

- **Nearest (adjective):** Closest in distance.
- **Next (adjective):** Following immediately in order or time.

Usage:

"Nearest" for proximity: *The nearest hospital is 5 km away.*

"Next" for sequence: *I'll be next in line.*

Example Sentences:

Where is the **nearest** bank?

The **next** bus arrives in 10 minutes.

Never or Not … Ever?

- **Never (adverb):** At no time; not at all.
- **Not … Ever (phrase):** Used to emphasise that something has not happened or will not happen.

Usage:

"Never" for no occurrences: *I have never been to Abuja.*

"Not ... Ever" for emphasis: *I will not ever go there again.*

Example Sentences:

Never give up on your dreams.

I will **not ever** forget your kindness.

Nice or Sympathetic?

- **Nice (adjective):** Pleasant, agreeable, or kind.
- **Sympathetic (adjective):** Showing understanding and care for someone else's feelings.

Usage:

"Nice" for general kindness: *She is a nice person.*

"Sympathetic" for understanding and care: *He was very sympathetic when I told him the bad news.*

Example Sentences:

The teacher is very **nice** to her students.

My friend was **sympathetic** when I lost my job.

No Doubt or Without Doubt?

- **No Doubt (phrase):** Used to indicate that something is very likely or certain.
- **Without Doubt (phrase):** Emphasises that something is absolutely certain.

Usage:

"No doubt" for likely certainty: *No doubt he will succeed.*

"Without doubt" for absolute certainty: *She is without doubt the best candidate.*

Example Sentences:

No doubt he will arrive soon.

Without doubt, this is the best movie I've seen this year.

No or Not?

- **No (adverb):** Used to give a negative response.
- **Not (adverb):** Used to form the negative of verbs, adjectives, and other adverbs.

Usage:

"No" to answer negatively: *No, I don't have any money.*

"Not" to negate verbs or adjectives: *I'm not going to the party.*

Example Sentences:

> **No**, I haven't finished my homework.
>
> I'm **not** interested in the job.

Nowadays, These Days or Today?

- **Nowadays (adverb):** At the present time, used to contrast with the past.
- **These Days (phrase):** Refers to the current period, often with a similar meaning to "nowadays."
- **Today (adverb/noun):** Refers to the current day or period.

Usage:

> "Nowadays" for general present time: *Nowadays, people use smartphones a lot.*
>
> "These days" for current trends: *These days, everyone seems to be on social media.*
>
> "Today" for the specific current day or period: *Today, I have a meeting.*

Example Sentences:

> **Nowadays**, cars are much more efficient.
>
> **These days**, it's hard to find time for hobbies.
>
> **Today** is a public holiday.

Open or Opened?

- **Open (adjective):** Not closed; available for use.
- **Opened (verb/adjective):** Past tense of "open," meaning something was made accessible.

Usage:

> "Open" as a state: *The shop is open.*
>
> "Opened" for past action: *I opened the window.*

Example Sentences:

> The door is **open**.
>
> She **opened** the letter quickly.

Opportunity or Possibility?

- **Opportunity (noun):** A set of circumstances that makes something possible.
- **Possibility (noun):** A chance that something may happen.

Usage:

"Opportunity" for favourable chances: *This job is a great opportunity.*

"Possibility" for potential events: *There is a possibility of rain tomorrow.*

Example Sentences:

He was given an **opportunity** to study abroad.

There's a **possibility** we might win the competition.

Opposite or In Front of?

- **Opposite (preposition/adjective):** Directly facing or on the other side.
- **In Front of (preposition):** Positioned before or ahead of something.

Usage:

"Opposite" for directly across: *The bank is opposite the park.*

"In front of" for something ahead: *The car is parked in front of the house.*

Example Sentences:

The school is **opposite** the market.

There's a bus stop **in front of** the mall.

Other, Others, The Other or Another?

- **Other (adjective):** Different or additional.
- **Others (pronoun):** Refers to additional people or things not specified.
- **The Other (phrase):** Refers to the second of two items.
- **Another (adjective):** An additional one of the same type.

Usage:

"Other" for something different: *Do you have any other questions?*

"Others" for additional people/things: *Some went to the party, others stayed home.*

"The other" for the second in a pair: *He took one, and I took the other.*

"Another" for one more: *Can I have another piece of cake?*

Example Sentences:

Do you want this one or the **other** one?

The **others** are still coming.

She picked one apple, and I took **the other**.

I need **another** pen.

Out or Out of?

- **Out (adverb/preposition):** Moving away from a place or point.
- **Out of (preposition):** Indicates movement from within something to the outside.

Usage:

"Out" for general movement away: *He went out.*

"Out of" for leaving an enclosure or container: *He walked out of the room.*

Example Sentences:

I'm going **out** tonight.

The cat jumped **out of** the box.

Permit or Permission?

- **Permit (verb/noun):** To allow something (verb); a document that allows something (noun).
- **Permission (noun):** The act of allowing someone to do something.

Usage:

"Permit" for allowing: *The city permits street parking.*

"Permission" for the act of allowing: *I need permission to leave early.*

Example Sentences:

You need a **permit** to build here.

She asked for **permission** to attend the event.

Person, Persons or People?

- **Person (noun):** An individual human being.
- **Persons (noun):** A formal or legal plural of "person."
- **People (noun):** The common plural of "person," referring to human beings collectively.

Usage:

"Person" for an individual: *There is one person in the room.*

"Persons" in formal/legal contexts: *All persons must vacate the premises.*

"People" for a group: *People are gathering for the event.*

Example Sentences:

He is a very kind **person**.

Persons with disabilities have special access.

The **people** in this city are very welcoming.

Pick or Pick Up?

- **Pick (verb):** To choose or select something.
- **Pick Up (phrasal verb):** To lift something or someone; also to collect.

Usage:

"Pick" for choosing: *Pick the best one.*

"Pick up" for lifting or collecting: *Can you pick up the package?*

Example Sentences:

Pick a colour for the walls.

I need to **pick up** the kids from school.

Play or Game?

- **Play (verb/noun):** Engage in an activity for enjoyment or recreation; a dramatic performance (noun).
- **Game (noun):** A structured form of play, often competitive, with rules.

Usage:

"Play" for engaging in activities: *Children love to play.*

"Game" for structured activities: *Football is a popular game.*

Example Sentences:

They like to **play** outside.

The **game** was very exciting.

Politics, Political, Politician or Policy?

- **Politics (noun):** The activities or affairs associated with government or decision-making.
- **Political (adjective):** Related to politics.
- **Politician (noun):** A person who is professionally involved in politics.
- **Policy (noun):** A course of action or principle adopted by a government, organization, or individual.

Usage:

"Politics" for the overall system or activities: *She is interested in politics.*

"Political" for matters relating to politics: *Political debates are common in elections.*

"Politician" for a person involved in politics: *He is a well-known politician.*

"Policy" for specific rules or guidelines: *The school has a strict attendance policy.*

Example Sentences:

Politics can be very complicated.

The **political** situation is tense.

The **politician** gave a speech on healthcare.

The company's **policy** on leave is very clear.

Price or Prize?

- **Price (noun):** The amount of money required to purchase something.
- **Prize (noun):** A reward given for a competition, achievement, or winning.

Usage:

"Price" for cost: *The price of the book is £10.*

"Prize" for a reward: *She won the first prize in the contest.*

Example Sentences:

What's the **price** of this laptop?

The **prize** for the winner is a trophy.

Principal or Principle?

- **Principal (noun/adjective):** The most important; the head of a school (noun).
- **Principle (noun):** A fundamental truth or proposition that serves as the foundation for a system of belief or behaviour.

Usage:

"Principal" for importance or school head: *The principal of the school is very strict.*

"Principle" for fundamental truths: *He is a man of principle.*

Example Sentences:

The **principal** reason for the delay is traffic.

The **principle** of fairness is essential in law.

Quiet or Quite?

- **Quiet (adjective):** Making little or no noise; calm.
- **Quite (adverb):** To a certain degree or extent; really or truly.

Usage:

"Quiet" for silence: *The library is very quiet.*

"Quite" for emphasis or degree: *I am quite tired today.*

Example Sentences:

The room was **quiet** during the exam.

It's **quite** cold outside.

Raise or Rise?

- **Raise (verb):** To lift or move something to a higher position; requires an object.
- **Rise (verb):** To move upward or increase; does not require an object.

Usage:

"Raise" for lifting something: *Please raise your hand if you have a question.*

"Rise" for increasing or going up: *The sun rises in the east.*

Example Sentences:

They decided to **raise** the flag.

The temperature is expected to **rise** tomorrow.

Remember or Remind?

- **Remember (verb):** To recall or bring to mind something from the past.
- **Remind (verb):** To cause someone to remember something.

Usage:

"Remember" for personal recollection: *I remember my first day at school.*

"Remind" for prompting someone else: *Please remind me to call my sister.*

Example Sentences:

Do you **remember** our trip to Abuja?

Can you **remind** me to send that email?

Right or Rightly?

- **Right (adjective/adverb):** Correct or accurate; used to express agreement or direction.

- **Rightly (adverb):** In a morally correct way; justly.

Usage:

> "Right" for correctness or direction: *Turn right at the junction.*
>
> "Rightly" for moral correctness: *He was rightly praised for his efforts.*

Example Sentences:

> You answered the question **right**.
>
> She was **rightly** concerned about the issue.

Rob or Steal?

- **Rob (verb):** To take something from someone by force or threat.
- **Steal (verb):** To take something without permission, typically secretly.

Usage:

> "Rob" when there is a direct victim: *He was robbed at gunpoint.*
>
> "Steal" for taking without permission: *Someone stole my wallet.*

Example Sentences:

> The bank was **robbed** last night.
>
> He **stole** my idea and claimed it was his.

Say or Tell?

- **Say (verb):** To speak words; usually does not require an indirect object.
- **Tell (verb):** To inform someone about something; usually requires an indirect object.

Usage:

> "Say" for speaking words: *He said he was tired.*
>
> "Tell" for informing someone: *Please tell me the truth.*

Example Sentences:

> What did she **say** to you?
>
> I'll **tell** you the story later.

So That or In Order That?

- **So That (conjunction):** Used to indicate purpose; more common in informal speech.
- **In Order That (conjunction):** A formal expression to indicate purpose.

Usage:

"So that" for informal purpose: *I studied hard so that I could pass the exam.*

"In order that" for formal purpose: *He spoke clearly in order that everyone could understand.*

Example Sentences:

I'll arrive early **so that** I can get a good seat.

She checked the report twice **in order that** no mistakes were made.

Sometimes or Sometime?

- **Sometimes (adverb):** Occasionally; at certain times but not always.

- **Sometime (adverb):** At an unspecified or indefinite time.

Usage:

"Sometimes" for occasional events: *Sometimes I go for a walk in the evening.*

"Sometime" for an unspecified time: *Let's meet sometime next week.*

Example Sentences:

I **sometimes** watch TV before bed.

We should catch up **sometime** soon.

Sound or Noise?

- **Sound (noun):** Anything that can be heard; a general term.

- **Noise (noun):** Unpleasant or disruptive sound.

Usage:

"Sound" for anything heard: *The sound of the rain is soothing.*

"Noise" for unpleasant or loud sounds: *The noise from the traffic is unbearable.*

Example Sentences:

The **sound** of the waves is calming.

There was a lot of **noise** during the construction.

Speak or Talk?

- **Speak (verb):** To say words or communicate verbally; often more formal.

- **Talk (verb):** To have a conversation or discuss; more informal.

Usage:

"Speak" for formal communication: *I will speak to the manager about this issue.*

"Talk" for informal conversations: *Let's talk after the meeting.*

Example Sentences:

He **spoke** about his experiences during the seminar.

We need to **talk** about the project.

Such or So?

- **Such (determiner/adjective):** Used to emphasise a quality or condition.
- **So (adverb):** Used to indicate the degree or extent of something.

Usage:

"Such" to emphasise nouns: *She is such a talented artist.*

"So" to emphasise adjectives or adverbs: *The cake was so delicious.*

Example Sentences:

It was **such** a lovely day.

He was **so** tired after the journey.

There, Their or They're?

- **There (adverb):** Refers to a place or position; also used to introduce a subject.
- **Their (possessive adjective):** Shows possession, meaning something belongs to "them."
- **They're (contraction):** A contraction of "they are."

Usage:

"There" for location or existence: *There is a book on the table.*

"Their" for possession: *That is their house.*

"They're" as a contraction: *They're coming to the party tonight.*

Example Sentences:

There is a new shop in town.

Their car is parked outside.

They're going on holiday next week.

Towards or Toward?

- **Towards (preposition):** Indicates direction or movement in the direction of something; more commonly used in British English.
- **Toward (preposition):** The same as "towards," but more commonly used in American English.

Usage:

Both "towards" and "toward" mean the same thing, so usage depends on the preferred form of English. In British English, use "towards": *She walked towards the door.*

Example Sentences:

He ran **towards** the bus stop to catch the bus.

Wait or Wait For?

- **Wait (verb):** To remain in a place until something happens; does not need an object.

- **Wait For (phrasal verb):** To stay in a place until a specific event, person, or thing arrives or happens.

Usage:

"Wait" on its own: *We'll have to wait.*

"Wait for" when expecting something: *I'm waiting for the bus.*

Example Sentences:

We'll **wait** here until you return.

I have to **wait for** my friend before we leave.

Wake, Wake Up or Awaken?

- **Wake (verb):** To stop sleeping; often used without "up" in phrases like "wake someone."

- **Wake Up (phrasal verb):** To stop sleeping and become alert; can be more informal.

- **Awaken (verb):** A formal way of saying "wake up," used less often in everyday speech.

Usage:

"Wake" for general waking: *Please wake me at 6 a.m.*

"Wake up" for becoming alert: *I wake up at 7 every day.*

"Awaken" for formal contexts: *She was awakened by a loud noise.*

Example Sentences:

Can you **wake** the kids early tomorrow?

I usually **wake up** before my alarm goes off.

He was **awakened** by the sound of the rain.

Who, Which, That

Who, which, and that are pronouns used to introduce clauses, but their usage depends on what they are referring to.

1. **Who** (Pronoun)

   Part of Speech: Pronoun

   Usage: Use **who** only when referring to humans. It connects a clause to a person or people.

   Example: *The teacher who lives next door is very kind.*

   Explanation: "Who" is correctly used here because it refers to a human subject, "the teacher."

2. **Which** (Pronoun)

   Part of Speech: Pronoun

   Usage: Use **which** when referring to non-human subjects like objects, animals, or abstract concepts. It usually introduces non-essential information.

   Example: *The book, which I borrowed from the library, is very interesting.*

   Explanation: "Which" is used here to refer to "the book," a non-human subject.

3. **That** (Pronoun)

   Part of Speech: Pronoun

   Usage: Use **that** when referring to both people and things, but only when the clause it introduces is essential to the sentence's meaning.

   Example: *The car that I bought last week is already having issues.*

   Explanation: "That" refers to "the car" and introduces an essential clause explaining which specific car is being talked about.

Summary:

- **Who** is for people.
- **Which** is for things and animals (when the information is extra).
- **That** can be used for both people and things (when the information is necessary).

Worth or Worthwhile?

- **Worth (noun/adjective):** The value or usefulness of something; used as an adjective to describe something valuable.

- **Worthwhile (adjective):** Worth the time, money, or effort spent; useful or important enough to be worth the time or effort.

Usage:

"Worth" to discuss value: *This book is worth reading.*

"Worthwhile" to describe something worth the effort: *The trip was really worthwhile.*

Example Sentences:

It's definitely **worth** the money to invest in a good education.

Helping others is always **worthwhile**.

How to say phone numbers in English

In English, phone numbers are usually said digit by digit, especially if they contain separate groupings. For example, the number **0801 234 5678** would be said as:

- *"Oh eight oh one, two three four, five six seven eight."*

Take note:

- Zero is often pronounced as *"oh"*, but can also be said as *"zero"* depending on personal or regional preferences.

- Phone numbers are typically broken into sections for easier recall and pronunciation. For example, ***0801 234 5678***

We often say "oh" for zero when reading phone numbers because it's just easier and quicker to say. Instead of saying "zero," which can feel a bit stiff, "oh" rolls off the tongue more naturally. For example, *0801* would usually be said as "oh eight oh one" instead of "zero eight zero one."

This practice actually has a bit of history. Even before phones were common, people would say "oh" when reading out numbers, like in years (e.g., "1905" as "nineteen oh five"). It just stuck around because it's casual and easy.

In more formal situations, though, like in technical fields or maths, people stick to "zero" because it's more precise. But for everyday things like phone numbers, "oh" works perfectly fine and is what most people use in conversation.

CONCLUSION

As you reach the end of *Professionally and Personally Polished*, I hope you feel inspired to embrace the ongoing journey of effective communication. The skills you have explored throughout this book are more than just tools; they are stepping stones to building stronger relationships and achieving your goals.

Embrace the principles you have learned, practise them in your daily interactions, and continue to refine your approach to communication. Your ability to express yourself clearly and confidently will open doors to new opportunities, both personally and professionally.

I encourage you to take what you have learned and put it into action, knowing that every conversation is a chance to connect and grow. Thank you for joining me on this journey towards becoming polished in every aspect of your life.